LEON TROTSKY ON THE TRADE UNIONS

PATHFINDER PRESS, INC., NEW YORK

CONTENTS

Second Edition, 1975

Copyright © 1969 by Pathfinder Press, Inc.
All rights reserved
Library of Congress Catalog Card Number 75-92904
ISBN 0-87348-451-7
Manufactured in the United States of America

Pathfinder Press, Inc.
410 West Street
New York, N.Y. 10014

PART I: COMMUNISM AND SYNDICALISM

Preface
by Farrell Dobbs

The subject of this pamphlet may be more or less new to readers just developing an interest in radical politics. Someone in that position, who sought a quick way of making a tentative comparison of the terms used in the title, might decide to look them up in a dictionary. In *Webster's New International* he would find these definitions:

"*Communism* . . . a social and political doctrine or movement based upon revolutionary Marxian socialism that interprets history as a relentless class war eventually to result everywhere in the victory of the proletariat and the social ownership of the means of production with relative social and economic equality for all and ultimately to lead to a classless society."

"*Syndicalism* . . . a revolutionary political movement that aims by the general strike and direct action of labor unions to overthrow parliamentary democracy and establish a corporate society with general control in the hands of trade unions and workers' cooperatives."

Both of these dry, abstract definitions imply a working-class struggle for power in order to transform society. But they leave a big gap regarding vital questions of how that revolutionary aim is to be accomplished. It is precisely on those questions that Leon Trotsky takes the subject out of the realm of abstract generalities and, in a series of articles, counterposes communist and syndicalist views in terms of class-struggle realities. These articles, written in polemical form, center largely around the political evolution of the French syndicalist leader Monatte, a one-time revolutionary whose policies led him onto a false course.

Trotsky puts the question of communism and syndicalism into historical perspective. Latter-day syndicalism, he explains, represents the arrested development and retrogression of an earlier tendency which had moved part way onto the revolutionary road. The early syndicalists, who organized themselves in opposition to policies that brought the trade unions into collaboration with the capitalist ruling class, constituted an embryo of a revolutionary workers' party. Their political weakness lay in wrong views about the nature of the state and the role of the party in the struggle for workers' power. From these shortcomings arose their mistakes in tactics, such as one-sided preoccupation with the general strike as the central instrument for the transformation of society.

4

Revolutionary syndicalism found its further development and completion in the rise of the Communist movement (symbolized by the Bolshevik Party, as guided by Lenin and Trotsky, which led the Russian workers to revolutionary victory in 1917). With this advance the workers were enabled to unify program, organization, and tactics through their own revolutionary party and to go forward in a struggle for state power.

Around the central theme of the vital role of the revolutionary party, Trotsky polemicizes against syndicalist misconceptions about the question of state power. He takes up the subject of bureaucratism in its various forms of manifestation within the labor movement. Readers in this country should especially note his comments about the reactionary character of the native trade union bureaucracy and the lessons to be derived from the role of similar formations abroad. Taken in context with his remarks about the myth of politically "independent" trade unions, the analysis sheds light on fundamental aspects of contemporary working-class politics.

This series of articles, written by a master polemicist who had exceptional Marxist insight into the laws of class struggle, appeared across the years 1923 to 1931. The period was marked by the rise of Stalinism in the world Communist movement. That caused Trotsky, as leader of the Left Opposition, to include in the series some pertinent material on Communist policy in the trade unions. Although the material relates specifically to earlier historical conditions, the basic concepts set forth retain full validity and constitute a valuable guide for worker-militants today.

An introduction to the first edition of this pamphlet was written in 1931 by James P. Cannon, founding leader of the Trotskyist movement in the United States. One of his concerns at the time was the skepticism in this country about the Communist movement among militants with a syndicalist background. He said to them: "But, granting serious defects in the party, what is to be done about it? As we see the thing—since we proceed from the point of view that a party cannot be dispensed with—one must either struggle to reform the party or, if he thinks it is hopeless, form a new one. We, the opposition, have taken the former course."

The policy he described of working to reform the Communist parties of the Third International was later changed by the Left Opposition. The turn came when Stalinism's false policy helped deliver the German workers into Hitler's hands in 1933. With that catastrophe it became clear that Stalinism had so bankrupted the Third International that its former revolutionary vitality could not be restored. The situation required the building of new national parties in opposition to the Stalinized Communist parties and the uniting of the reconstructed parties into a new revolutionary international.

This new course led in 1938 to the launching of the Fourth International and, in this country, to the formation of the Socialist Workers Party. Although prevented by antidemocratic legislation from belonging to the Fourth International, the Socialist Workers Party shares its general political outlook.

(Later on Cannon wrote a pamphlet about the syndicalists of the IWW in which he drew the lessons of their experiences. In a separate but broadly interrelated work, he made a study of the early socialist movement centered around Eugene V. Debs. These two pamphlets contribute greatly to an understanding of the perspectives and problems involved in building a revolutionary working-class party.*)

Syndicalism is not a significant tendency within this country's trade unions today, but there are notions of a comparable nature within the "New Left." These notions stem from blind and sweeping rejection of the "Old Left" and, along with it, all the hard-won historical lessons about the decisive role of a Bolshevik-type party. This leads to improvisations of policy and action that can only wind up repeating the syndicalist mistakes of the past.

Attempts to turn the clock back by reviving syndicalist-type views can have only reactionary significance for the labor and radical movement. Trotsky shows why in practice that would mean the dissolution of the revolutionary vanguard into the politically backward mass of the broad, amorphous trade unions. Such a course contradicts the workers' need for conscious guidance on firmly established principles. It cuts across the task of forging the necessary leadership by uniting vanguard elements in the party of the proletarian revolution. As history has proven, a disciplined combat party is the only instrument that can stand against the organized opposition of the capitalist ruling class and its repressive apparatus, the state.

*　　*　　*

The first two articles in *Communism and Syndicalism* were written in 1923 shortly after Pierre Monatte and his revolutionary syndicalist group had joined the Communist Party of France. The next two, written in 1929, take up the discussion again six years later, when Monatte was retreating to his old position and away from communism. The fifth, in 1930, draws a balance sheet of the discussion with the syndicalists after their bloc with a reformist wing of the union movement. The sixth article, in 1931, deals with problems of Marxist policy in the unions then being discussed by the French section of the International Left Opposition. *Communism and Syndicalism* was first published in the United States in March, 1931, by the Militant Press, with a translation by Max Shachtman, which has been slightly revised for the present edition.

---

* Both are reprinted in Cannon's *First Ten Years of American Communism* (Pathfinder 1973).

A Necessary Discussion
With Our Syndicalist Comrades

This article was written as a reply to the arguments of Comrade Louzon, [1] immediately after the Fourth World Congress of the Communist International. [2] But at that time, more attention was being devoted to the struggle against the socialist right, against the last batch of dissidents, Verfeuil, Frossard, etc. [3] In this struggle our efforts were, and continue to be, united with those of the syndicalists, and I preferred to postpone the publication of this article. We are firmly convinced that our excellent understanding with the revolutionary syndicalists will not cease to exist. The entrance of our old friend Monatte [4] into the Communist Party was a great day for us. The revolution needs men of this kind. But it would be wrong to pay for a *rapprochement* with a confusion of ideas. In the course of recent months, the Communist Party of France has been purified and consolidated; hence we can enter into a tranquil and friendly discussion with our syndicalist comrades, side by side with whom we shall have much work to do and many battles to fight.

Comrade Louzon, in a series of articles and personal explanations, represented views with regard to the fundamental question of the relations between party and trade union which differ radically from the opinions of the Communist International and from Marxism. French comrades whose opinion I am accustomed to respect speak with great esteem of Comrade Louzon and his devotion to the proletariat. It is all the more necessary, therefore, to correct the errors made by him in such an important question. Comrade Louzon defends the complete and unqualified independence of the trade unions. Against what? Obviously against certain attacks. Whose? Against attacks ascribed to the party. Trade union autonomy, an indisputable necessity, is endowed with a certain absolute and almost mystical significance by Louzon. And our comrade here appeals, quite wrongly, to Marx.

The trade unions, says Louzon, represent the "working class as a whole." The party, however, is only a party. The working class as a whole cannot be subordinated to the party. There is not even room for equality between them. "The working class has its aim in itself." The party, however, can only either serve the working class or be subordinated to it. Thus the party cannot "annex" the working class. The mutual representation of the Communist International and the

Red International of Labor Unions,[5] which existed until the last Moscow congresses, signify, according to Louzon, the actual equalization of party and class. This mutual representation has now been abolished. The party thereby resumes its role of servant again. Comrade Louzon approves of this. According to him, this was also the standpoint of Marx. The end of the mutual representation of the political and trade union internationals in each other is, to Louzon, the rejection of the errors of Lassalle (!)[6] and of the social democrats (!) and a return to the principles of Marxism.

This is the essence of an article that appeared in the *Vie ouvrière* [7] of December 15. The most astonishing thing in this and other similar articles is that the writer is obviously, consciously and determinedly, shutting his eyes to what is actually going on in France. One might think that the article had been written from the star Sirius. How else is it possible to understand the assertion that the trade unions represent the "working class as a whole"? Of what country is Louzon talking? If he means France, the trade unions there, so far as we are informed, do not, unfortunately, include even half of the working class. The criminal maneuvers of the reformist trade unionists, supported on the left by some few anarchists, have split the French trade union organization. Neither of the two trade union confederations embraces more than 300,000 workers. Neither singly nor together are they entitled to identify themselves with the whole of the French proletariat, of which they form only a modest part. Moreover, each trade union organization pursues a different policy. The reformist trade union confederation [*Confédération Générale du Travail (CGT)*] works in cooperation with the bourgeoisie; the Unitary General Confederation of Labor [*Confédération Générale du Travail Unitaire (CGTU)*] is, fortunately, revolutionary. In the latter organization, Louzon represents but one tendency. What then does he mean by the assertion that the working class, which he obviously regards as synonymous with the trade union organization, bears its own aim in itself? With whose help, and how, does the French working class express this aim? With the help of Jouhaux's [8] organization? Certainly not. With the help of the CGTU? The CGTU has already rendered great services. But unfortunately it is not yet the whole working class. Finally, to mention everything, it was not so long ago that the CGTU was led by the anarcho-syndicalists of the "Pact."[9] At the present time its leaders are syndicalist communists. In which of these two periods has the CGTU best represented the interests of the working class? Who is to judge? If we now attempt, with the aid of the international experience of *our party*, to answer this question, then, in Louzon's opinion, we commit a mortal sin, for we then demand that the party judge what policy is most beneficial to the working class. That is, we place the party above the working class. But if we were to turn to the *working class as a whole*, we would unfortunately find it divided, impotent, and mute. The different parts of the class organized into different confederations, even different trade unions in the same confederation, and even different groups in the same trade union, would all give us different replies. But the overwhelming majority of the proletariat, standing outside both trade union confederations, would, at the present time, give us no reply at all.

There is no country in which the trade union organization embraces the whole working class. But in some countries it at least comprises a very large section of the workers. This is, however, not the case in France. If, as Louzon opines, the party must not "annex" the working class (what is this term actually supposed to mean?), then for what reason does Comrade Louzon accord this right to syndicalism? He may reply: "Our trade union organization is still weak. But we do not doubt its future and its final victory." To this we should reply: "Certainly; we too share this conviction. But we have just as little doubt that the party too will win the unqualified confidence of the great majority of the working class." Neither for the party nor for the trade unions is it a question of "annexing" the proletariat—it is wrong for Louzon to employ the terminology customarily used by our opponents in their fight against the revolution—it is a question of *winning the confidence* of the proletariat. And it is only possible to do this with correct tactics, tested by experience. Where and by whom are these tactics consciously, carefully, and critically prepared? Who suggests them to the working class? Certainly they do not fall from heaven. And the working class as a whole, as a "thing in itself," does not teach us these tactics either. It seems to us that Comrade Louzon has not faced this question.

"The proletariat has its aim within itself." If we strip this sentence of its mystical trappings, its obvious meaning is that the historical tasks of the proletariat are determined by its social position as a class and by its role in production, in society, and in the state. This is beyond dispute. But this truth does not help us answer the question with which we are concerned, namely: How is the proletariat to arrive at *subjective insight* into the historical task posed by its objective position? Were the proletariat as a whole capable of grasping its historical task immediately, it would need neither party nor trade union. Revolution would be born simultaneously with the proletariat. But in actuality the *process* by which the proletariat gains an insight into its historic mission is very long and painful, and full of internal contradictions.

It is only in the course of long struggles, severe trials, many vacillations, and extensive experience, that insight as to the right ways and methods dawns upon the minds of the best elements of the working class, the vanguard of the masses. This applies equally to party and trade union. The trade union also begins as a small group of active workers and grows gradually as its experience enables it to gain the confidence of the masses. But while the revolutionary organizations are struggling to gain influence in the working class, the bourgeois ideologists counterpose the "working class as a whole" not only against the party of the working class but against its trade unions, which these ideologists accuse of wanting to "annex" the working class. *Le Temps* [10] writes this whenever there is a strike. In other words, the bourgeois ideologists counterpose the working class as object to the working class as conscious subject. For it is only through its class-conscious minority that the working class gradually becomes a factor in history. We thus see that the criticism leveled by Comrade Louzon against the "unwarranted claims" of the party *applies equally well to the "unwarranted claims" of the trade unions.* Above all in France, for French syndicalism — we must repeat this — was and is, in its organization and theory, likewise a *party*. This is also why it arrived, during its classic period (1905-07), at the theory of the "active minority," and not at the theory of the "collective proletariat." For what else is an active minority, held together by the unity of their ideas, if not a party? And on the other hand, would not a trade union mass organization, not containing a class-conscious active minority, be a purely formal and meaningless organization?

The fact that French syndicalism was a *party* was fully confirmed by the split which took place as soon as divergences in political viewpoints appeared in its ranks. But the party of revolutionary syndicalism fears the aversion felt by the French working class for parties as such. Therefore it has not assumed the *name* of party and has remained incomplete as regards organization. It is a party that attempted to have its members blend into the trade union membership, or at least take cover behind the trade unions. The actual subordination of the trade unions to certain tendencies, factions, and even cliques of syndicalism is thus explained. This is also the explanation of the "Pact," which is a masonic caricature of a party within the bosom of the trade union organization. And vice versa: the Communist International has most determinedly combated the split in the trade union movement in France, that is, its actual conversion into syndicalist parties. The main consideration of the Communist International has been the historical task of the working class as a whole, and the enormous independent significance of the trade union organization for solving the tasks of the proletariat. In this respect, the Communist International has from its very inception defended the real and living independence of the trade unions, in the spirit of Marxism.

Revolutionary syndicalism, which was in France in many respects the precursor of present-day Communism, has acknowledged the theory of the active minority, that is, of the party, but without openly becoming a party. It has thereby prevented the trade unions from becoming if not an organization of the whole working class (which is not possible in a capitalist system), at least of its broad masses. The Communists are not afraid of the word "party," for their party has nothing in common, and will have nothing in common, with the other parties. Their party is not one of the political parties of the bourgeois system; it is the active, class-conscious minority of the proletariat, its revolutionary vanguard. Hence the Communists have no reason, either in their ideology or their organization, to hide themselves behind the trade unions. They do not misuse the trade unions for machinations behind the scenes. They do not split the trade unions when they are a minority in them. They do not in any way disturb the independent development of the trade unions, and they support trade union struggles with all their strength. But at the same time the Communist Party reserves the right of expressing its opinion on all questions in the working-class movement, including the trade union question, to criticize trade union tactics, and to make definite proposals to the trade unions, which, on their part, are at liberty to accept or reject these proposals. The party strives to win the confidence of the working class, above all, of that section organized in the trade unions.

What is the meaning of the quotations from Marx adduced by Comrade Louzon? It is a fact that Marx wrote in 1868 that the workers' party would emerge from the trade union. When writing this he was thinking mainly of England, at that time the sole developed capitalist country already possessing extensive labor organizations. Half a century has passed since then. Historical experience has in general confirmed Marx's prophecies insofar as England is concerned. The English Labour Party has actually been built up on the foundation of the trade unions. But does Comrade Louzon really think that the English Labour Party, as it is today, led by Henderson and Clynes, can be looked upon as representative of the interests of the proletariat as a whole? Most decidedly not. The Labour Party in Great Britain betrays the cause of the proletariat just as the trade union bureaucracy betrays it, although in England the trade unions come closer to comprising the working class as a whole than anywhere else. On the other hand, we cannot doubt but that our Communist influence will grow in this English Labour Party which emerged from the trade unions, and that this will contribute to render more acute the struggle between the masses and leaders within the trade unions until the treacherous bureaucrats are ultimately driven forth and the Labour Party is completely transformed and regenerated. And we, like Comrade Louzon, belong to an International which includes the little British Communist Party, but which combats the Second International supported by the English Labour Party that had its origin in the trade unions.

In Russia — and in the law of capitalist development Russia is just the antipode of Great Britain — the Communist Party, the former social-democratic party, is older than the trade unions, and created the trade unions. Today, the trade unions and the workers' state in Russia are completely under the influence of the Communist Party, which by no means had its origin in the trade unions but which, on the contrary, created and trained them. Will Comrade Louzon contend that Russia has evolved in contradiction to Marxism? Is it not simpler to say that Marx's judgment on the origin of the party in the trade union has been proved by experience to have been correct for England, and even there not 100 per cent correct, but that Marx never had the least intention of laying down what he himself once scornfully designated as a "supra-historical law"? All the other countries of Europe, including France, stand between Great Britain and Russia on this question. In some countries the trade unions are older than the party, in others the contrary has been the case; but nowhere, except in England and partially in Belgium, has the party of the proletariat emerged from the trade unions. In any case, no Communist party has developed organically out of the trade unions. But are we to deduce from this that the entire Communist International is of illegitimate birth?

When the English trade unions alternately supported the Conservatives and the Liberals and represented to a certain extent a labor appendage to these parties, when the political organization of the German workers was nothing more than a left wing of the democratic party, when the followers of Lassalle and Eisenach [11] were quarreling among themselves—Marx demanded the independence of the trade unions from all parties. This formula was dictated by the desire to counterpose the labor organizations to all bourgeois parties, and to prevent their being too closely bound up with socialist sects. But Comrade Louzon may perhaps remember that it was Marx who founded the First International as well, the object of which was to guide the labor movement in all countries, in every respect, and to render it fruitful. This was in 1864 and *the International created by Marx was a party.* Marx refused to wait until the international party of the working class formed itself in some way out of the trade unions. He did his utmost to strengthen, within the trade unions, the influence of the ideas of scientific socialism—ideas first expressed in 1847 in the *Communist Manifesto.* When Marx demanded for the trade unions complete independence from all existing parties and sects, that is, from all the bourgeois and petty bourgeois parties and sects, he did this in order to make it easier for scientific socialism to gain dominance in the trade unions. Marx never saw in the party of scientific socialism one of the existing political parties (parliamentary, democratic, etc.). For Marx the International was the class-conscious working class, represented at that time by a still very small vanguard.

If Comrade Louzon were consistent in his trade union metaphysic and in his interpretation of Marx, he would say, "Let us renounce the Communist Party and wait till this party arises out of the trade unions." That kind of logic would be fatal, not only for the party but for the union. Actually, the present French trade unions can only regain their unity and win decisive influence over the masses if their best elements are constituted in the class-conscious revolutionary vanguard of the proletariat, that is, in a Communist Party. Marx gave no final answer to the question of the relations between party and trade unions, and indeed he could not do so. For these relations are dependent on the varying circumstances in each separate case. Whether the party and the trade union confederation are mutually represented on their central committees, or whether they form joint committees of action as needed, is a question of no decisive importance. The forms of organization may alter, but the fundamental role of the party remains constant. The party, if it be worthy of the name, includes the whole vanguard of the working class and uses its ideological influence for rendering every branch of the labor movement fruitful, especially the trade union movement. But if the trade unions are worthy of their name, they include an ever growing mass of workers, many backward elements among them. But they can only fulfill their task when consciously guided on firmly established principles. And they can only have this leadership when their best elements are united in the party of proletarian revolution.

The recent purification of the Communist Party of France, which rid itself on the one hand of whining petty bourgeois, of drawing-room heroes, of political Hamlets and sickening careerists, and on the other hand actuated the *rapprochement* of Communists and revolutionary syndicalists, implies a great stride towards the creation of suitable relations between trade union organizations and the political organization, which in turn means a great advance for the revolution.

March 23, 1923

The Anarcho-Syndicalist Prejudices Again!

Comrade Louzon's new article [12] contains more errors than his earlier ones, although this time his main line of argument takes an entirely different turn.

In his former articles, Comrade Louzon's starting points were abstractions which assumed that the trade unions represented the "working class as a whole." In my reply I put the question: "Where does Comrade Louzon write his articles — in France or on Sirius?" In his latest article Comrade Louzon deserts the shaky foundation of universal laws and attempts to stand upon the national ground of French syndicalism. Yes, he says, the French trade unions are not actually the working class as a whole, but only the active minority of the working class. That is, Comrade Louzon acknowledges that the trade unions form a sort of revolutionary party. But this syndicalist party is distinguished by being purely proletarian in it constituents; here lies its tremendous advantage over the Communist Party. And it has still another advantage: the syndicalist party categorically rejects the bourgeois state institutions; it does not "recognize" democracy, and thus takes no part in the parliamentary struggles.

Comrade Louzon is never weary of repeating that we are dealing with the peculiarities of French development, and with these only. Beginning with a broad generalization, in the course of which he transformed Marx into a syndicalist, Louzon now sets England, Russia, and Germany apart. He does not reply to our question on why he himself belongs to the Communist International, in company with the small English Communist Party, and not to the Second International, in company with the English trade unions and the English Labour Party which is supported by them. Louzon began with a "supra-historical" law for all countries, and closes by claiming an exceptional law for France. In this new form Louzon's theory bears a purely national character. More than this, its essential character excludes the possibility of an International: How can common tactics be spoken of unless there are common fundamental premises? It is certainly very difficult to understand why Comrade Louzon belongs to the Communist International. It is no less difficult to understand why he belongs to the French Communist Party, since there exists another party possessing all the advantages of the Communist and none of its drawbacks.

But though Comrade Louzon leaves international ground for the sake of national, he systematically ignores that "national" question put to him in our former article: What about the role played by the CGT [13] during the war? The role played by Jouhaux was by no means less treacherous and despicable than that played by Renaudel. [14] The sole difference consisted in the fact that the social patriotic party arranged its views and actions in accordance with a cerain system, while the trade union patriots acted purely empirically and veiled their actions in wretched and stupid improvisations. It may be said that, as regards patriotic betrayal, the socialist party, with its definite character, surpassed the semidefinite syndicalist party. At bottom, Jouhaux was at one with Renaudel.

And how is it today? Does Louzon desire the union of the two confederations? We desire it. The International deems it necessary. We should not be alarmed even if the union were to give Jouhaux the majority. Naturally we would not say — as does Comrade Louzon — that syndicalism, although headed by Jouhaux, Dumoulin, Merrheim and their like,[15] is the purest form of proletarian organization, that it embodies "the working class as a whole," etc., etc. — for such a phrase would be a travesty of the facts. But we should consider the formation of a larger trade union organization, that is, the concentration of greater proletarian masses, forming a wider battlefield for the struggle for the ideas and tactics of Communism, to be a greater gain for the cause of revolution. But for this the first necessity is that the ideas and tactics of Communism do not remain in midair, but are organized in the form of a party. With regard to Comrade Louzon, he does not pursue his thoughts to the end, but his logical conclusion would be the substitution of the party by a trade union organization of the "active minority." The inevitable result of this would be a substitute party and substitute trade union, for those trade unions required by Comrade Louzon are too indefinite for the role of a party, and too small for the role of a trade union.

Comrade Louzon's arguments to the effect that the trade unions do not want to soil their fingers by contact with the organs of bourgeois democracy, already form a weak echo of anarchism. It may be assumed that the majority of the workers organized in the CGTU will vote at the elections for the Communist Party (at least we hope that Comrade Louzon, as a member of the Communist Party, will call upon them to do so), while the majority of the members of the yellow confederation will vote for the Blum-Renaudel party. [16] The trade union, as a form of organization, is not adapted for parliamentary struggle, but the workers organized in the trade unions will nevertheless have their deputies. It is simply a case of division of labor on the same class foundation. Or is it perchance a matter of indifference to the French worker what happens in parliament? The workers do not think so. The trade unions have frequently reacted to the legislative work of parliament, and will continue to do so in the future. And if there are, at the same time, Communist deputies in parliament itself, who work hand in hand with the revolutionary trade unions against the deeds of violence and blows of imperialist "democracy," this is naturally a plus and not a minus. French "tradition" says that deputies are traitors. But the Communist Party has been called into being for the express purpose of doing away with all tradition. Should any deputy think of retreating from the class line, he will be thrown out of the party. Our French party has learned how to do this, and all distrust in it is completely unfounded.

But Louzon complains that the party contains many petty-bourgeois intellectuals. This is so. But the Fourth Congress of the Communist International recognized and adopted resolutions on this, and the resolutions have not been without effect. Further work is required to establish the proletarian character of the party. But we shall not attain this end with the self-contradictory trade union metaphysics of Comrade Louzon, but rather by means of systematic party work in the sphere of the trade unions, and in every other sphere of proletarian struggle. There is already a considerable number of workers in the Central Committee of our French party. This is mirrored in the whole party. The same tendency is at work, in accordance with the resolutions passed by the Fourth Congress, in the parliamentary and municipal elections. By this the party will win the confidence of the revolutionary proletariat. And this means that the party will less and less lack really competent and active proletarians to occupy the most important and responsible revolutionary posts. I greatly fear that Comrade Louzon's views may exercise a retarding influence on this profound progressive evolution of the vanguard of the French working class. But I have no doubt that Communism will succeed in overcoming this obstacle, like all others.

Moscow, May 8, 1923.

Communism and Syndicalism

The trade union question is one of the most important for the labor movement and, consequently, for the Opposition. Without a precise position on the trade union question, the Opposition will be unable to win real influence upon the working class. That is why I believe it necessary to submit here, *for discussion,* a few considerations on the trade union question.

1. The Communist Party is the fundamental weapon of revolutionary action of the proletariat, the combat organization of its vanguard that must raise itself to the role of leader of the working class in all the spheres of its struggle without exception, and consequently, in the trade union field.

2. Those who, in principle, counterpose trade union autonomy to the leadership of the Communist Party, counterpose thereby — whether they want to or not — the most backward proletarian section to the vanguard of the working class, the struggle for immediate demands to the struggle for the complete liberation of the workers, reformism to Communism, opportunism to revolutionary Marxism.

3. Prewar French syndicalism, at the epoch of its rise and expansion, by fighting for trade union autonomy actually fought for its independence from the bourgeois government and its parties, among them that of reformist-parliamentary socialism. This was a struggle against opportunism — for a revolutionary road.

Revolutionary syndicalism did not, in this connection, make a fetish of the autonomy of the mass organizations. On the contrary, it understood and preached the leading role of the revolutionary minority in relation to the mass organizations, which reflect the working class with all its contradictions, its backwardness, and its weaknesses.

4. The theory of the active minority was, in essence, an uncompleted theory of a proletarian party. In all its practice, revolutionary syndi-

calism was an embryo of a revolutionary party as against opportunism, that is, it was a remarkable draft outline of revolutionary Communism.

5. The weakness of anarcho-syndicalism, even in its classic period, was the absence of a correct theoretical foundation, and, as a result, a wrong understanding of the nature of the state and its role in the class struggle; an incomplete, not fully developed and, consequently, a wrong conception of the role of the revolutionary minority, that is, the party. Thence the mistakes in tactics, such as the fetishism of the general strike, the ignoring of the connection between the uprising and the seizure of power, etc.

6. After the war, French syndicalism found not only its refutation but also its development and its completion in Communism. Attempts to revive revolutionary syndicalism now would be to try and turn back history. For the labor movement, such attempts can have only reactionary significance.

7. The epigones [17] of syndicalism transform (in words) the independence of the trade union organization from the bourgeoisie and the reformist socialists into *independence in general,* into *absolute* independence from all parties, the Communist included.

If, in the period of expansion, syndicalism considered itself a vanguard and fought for the leading role of the vanguard minority among the backward masses, the epigones of syndicalism now fight against the identical wishes of the Communist vanguard, attempting, even though without success, to base themselves upon the lack of development and the prejudices of the more backward sections of the working class.

8. Independence from the influence of the bourgeoisie cannot be a passive state. It can express itself only by political acts, that is, by the struggle against the bourgeoisie. This struggle must be inspired by a distinct program which requires organization and tactics for its application. It is the union of program, organization, and tactics that constitutes the party. In this way, the real independence of the proletariat from the bourgeois government cannot be realized unless the proletariat conducts its struggle under the leadership of a revolutionary and not an opportunist party.

9. The epigones of syndicalism would have one believe that the trade unions are sufficient by themselves. Theoretically, this means nothing, but in practice it means the dissolution of the revolutionary vanguard into the backward masses, that is, the trade unions.

The larger the mass the trade unions embrace, the better they are able to fulfill their mission. A proletarian party, on the contrary, merits its name only if it is ideologically homogeneous, bound by unity of action and organization. To represent the trade unions as self-sufficient because the proletariat has already attained its "majority," is to flatter the proletariat, is to picture it other than it is and can be under capitalism, which keeps enormous masses of workers in ignorance and backwardness, leaving only the vanguard of the proletariat the possibility of breaking through all the difficulties and arriving at a clear comprehension of the tasks of its class as a whole.

10. The real, practical and not the metaphysical autonomy of trade union organization is not in the least disturbed nor is it diminished by the struggle of the Communist Party for influence. Every member of the trade union has the right to vote as he thinks necessary and to elect the one who seems to him most worthy. Communists possess this right in the same way as others.

The conquest of the majority by the Communists in the directing organs takes place quite in accordance with the principles of autonomy, that is, the self-administration of the trade unions. On the other hand, no trade union statute can prevent or prohibit the party from electing the general secretary of the Confederation of Labor to its central committee, for here we are entirely in the domain of the autonomy of the party.

11. In the trade unions, the Communists, of course, submit to the discipline of the party, no matter what posts they occupy. This does not exclude but presupposes their submission to trade union discipline. In other words, the party does not impose upon them any line of conduct that contradicts the state of mind or the opinions of the majority of the members of trade unions. In entirely exceptional cases, when the party considers impossible the submission of its members to some *reactionary* decision of the trade union, it points out openly to its members the consequences that flow from it, that is, removals from trade union posts, expulsions, and so forth.

With juridical formulas in these questions — and autonomy is a purely juridical formula — one can get nowhere. The question must be posed in its essence, that is, on the plane of trade union *policy*. A corect policy must be counterposed to a wrong policy.

12. The character of the party's leadership, its methods and its forms, can differ profoundly in accordance with the general conditions of a given country or with the period of its development.

In capitalist countries, where the Communist Party does not possess any means of coercion, it is obvious that it can give leadership only by Communists being in the trade unions as rank-and-file members or functionaries.

The number of Communists in leading posts of the trade unions is only one of the means of measuring the role of the party in the trade unions. The most important measurement is the percentage of rank-and-file Communists in relation to the whole unionized mass. But the principal criterion is the general influence of the party on the working class, which is measured by the circulation of the Communist press, the attendance at meetings of the party, the number of votes at elections and, what is especially important, the number of working men and women who respond actively to the party's appeals to struggle.

13. It is clear that the influence of the Communist Party in general, including the trade unions, will grow, the more revolutionary the situation becomes.

These conditions permit an appreciation of the degree and the form of the true, real and not the metaphysical autonomy of the trade unions. In times of "peace," when the most militant forms of trade union action are isolated economic strikes, the *direct* role of the party in trade union action falls back to second place. As a general rule, the party does not make a decision on every isolated strike. It *helps* the trade union to decide the question of knowing if the strike is opportune, by means of its political and economic information and by its advice. It *serves* the strike with its agitation, etc. First place in the strike belongs, of course, to the trade union.

The situation changes radically when the movement rises to the general strike and still more to the direct struggle for power. In these conditions, the leading role of the party becomes entirely direct, open, and immediate. The trade unions — naturally not those that pass over to the other side of the barricades — become the organizational apparatus of the party which, in the presence of the whole class, stands forth as the leader of the revolution, bearing the full responsibility.

In the field extending between the partial economic strike and the revolutionary class insurrection are placed all the possible forms of reciprocal relations between the party and the trade unions, the varying degrees of direct and immediate leadership, etc.

But under all conditions, the party seeks to win general leadership by relying upon the real autonomy of the trade unions which, as organizations — it goes without saying — are not "submitted" to it.

14. Facts show that politically "independent" unions do not exist anywhere. There never have been any. Experience and theory say that there never will be any. In the United States, the trade unions are directly bound by their apparatus to the general staffs of industry and the bourgeois parties. In England the trade unions, which in the past mainly supported the Liberals, now constitute the material basis of the Labour Party. In Germany, the trade unions march under the banner of the social democracy. In the Soviet republic, their leadership belongs to the Bolsheviks. In France, one of the trade union organizations follows the socialists, the other the Communists. In Finland, the trade unions were divided only a little while ago, one going towards the social democracy, the other towards Communism. That is how it is everywhere.

The theoreticians of the "independence" of the trade union movement have not taken the trouble up to now to think of this question: why their slogan not only does not approach its realization in practice anywhere, but why, on the contrary, the dependence of the trade unions upon the leadership of a party becomes everywhere, without exception, more and more evident and open. Yet, this corresponds entirely to the character of the imperialist epoch, which bares all class relations and which, even within the proletariat, accentuates the contradictions between its aristocracy and its most exploited sections.

15. The consummate expression of outdated syndicalism is the so-called Syndicalist League (*Ligue Syndicaliste*). By all its traits, it comes forward as a political organization which seeks to subordinate the trade union movement to its influence. In fact, the League recruits its members not in accordance with the trade union principle, but in accordance with the principle of political groupings; it has its platform, if not its program, and it defends it in its publications; it has its own internal discipline within the trade union movement. In the congresses of the Confederations, its partisans act as a political faction in the same way as the Communist faction. If we are not to lose ourselves in words, the tendency of the Syndicalist League reduces itself to a struggle to liberate the two Confederations from the leadership of the socialists and Communists and to unite them under the direction of the Monatte group.

The League does not act openly in the name of the right and the necessity for the advanced minority to fight to extend its influence over the most backward masses; it presents itself masked by what it calls trade union "independence." From this point of view, the League approaches the Socialist Party which also realizes its leadership under cover of the phrase "independence of the trade union movement." The Communist Party, on the contrary, says openly to the working class: here is my program, my tactics and my policy, which I propose to the trade unions.

The proletariat must never believe anything blindly. It must judge every party and every organization by its work. But the workers should have a double and triple distrust toward those pretenders to leadership who act incognito, under a mask who make the proletariat believe that it has no need of leadership in general.

16. The right of a political party to fight to win the trade unions to its influence must not be denied, but this question must be posed: In the name of what program and what tactics is this organization fighting? From this point of view, the Syndicalist League does not give the necessary guarantees. Its program is extremely amorphous, as are its tactics. In its political evaluations it acts only from event to event. Acknowledging the proletarian revolution and even the dictatorship of the proletariat, it ignores the party and fights against Communist leadership, without which the proletarian revolution would always risk remaining an empty phrase.

17. The ideology of trade union independence has nothing in common with the ideas and sentiments of the proletariat as a class. If the party, by its direction, is capable of assuring a correct, clear-sighted,

and firm policy in the trade unions, not a single worker will have the idea of rebelling against the leadership of the party. The historical experience of the Bolsheviks has proved that.

This also holds good for France, where the Communists received 1,200,000 votes in the elections while the *Confédération Générale du Travail Unitaire* (the central organization of the Red trade unions) has only a fourth or a third of this number. It is clear that the abstract slogan of independence can under no condition come from the masses. Trade union bureaucracy is quite another thing. It not only sees professional competition in the party bureaucracy, but it even tends to make itself independent of control by the vanguard of the proletariat. The slogan of independence is, by its very basis, a bureaucratic and not a class slogan.

18. After the fetish of "independence" the Syndicalist League also transforms the question of *trade union unity* into a fetish.

It goes without saying that the maintenance of the unity of the trade union organizations has enormous advantages, from the point of view of the daily tasks of the proletariat as well as from the point of view of the struggle of the Communist Party to extend its influence over the masses. But the facts prove that since the first successes of the revolutionary wing in the trade unions, the opportunists have set themselves deliberately on the road of split. Peaceful relations with the bourgeoisie are dearer to them than the unity of the proletariat. That is the indubitable summary of the postwar experiences.

We Communists are in every way interested in proving to the workers that the responsibility for the splitting of the trade union organizations falls wholly upon the social democracy. But it does not at all follow that the hollow formula of unity is more important for us than the revolutionary tasks of the working class.

19. Eight years have passed since the trade union split in France. During this time, the two organizations linked themselves definitely with the two mortally hostile political parties. Under these conditions, to think of being able to unify the trade union movement by the simple preaching of unity would be to nurture illusions. To declare that without the preliminary unification of the two trade union organizations not only the proletarian revolution but even a serious class struggle is impossible, means to make the future of the revolution depend upon the corrupted clique of trade union reformists.

In fact, the future of the revolution depends not upon the fusion of the two trade union apparatuses, but upon the unification of the majority of the working class around revolutionary slogans and revolutionary methods of struggle.

At present, the unification of the working class is only possible by fighting against the class collaborationists (coalitionists) who are found not only in political parties but also in the trade unions.

20. The real road to the revolutionary unity of the proletariat lies

in the development, the correction, the enlargement and consolidation of the revolutionary CGTU and in the weakening of the reformist CGT.

It is not excluded but, on the contrary, very likely that at the time of its revolution, the French proletariat will enter the struggle with two Confederations: behind one will be found the masses and behind the other the aristocracy of labor and the bureaucracy.

21. The new trade union opposition obviously does not want to enter on the road of syndicalism. At the same time, it breaks with the party — not with a certain leadership, but with the party in general. This means quite simply that ideologically it definitely disarms itself and falls back to the positions of craft or trade unionism.

22. The trade union opposition as a whole is very variegated. But it is characterized by some common features which do not bring it closer to the Left Communist Opposition but, on the contrary, alienate it and oppose it.

The trade union opposition does not fight against the thoughtless acts and wrong methods of the Communist leadership, but against the influence of Communism over the working class.

The trade union opposition does not fight against the ultraleftist evaluation of the given situation and the tempo of its development but acts, in reality, counter to revolutionary perspectives in general.

The trade union opposition does not fight against caricatured methods of antimilitarism but puts forward a pacifist orientation. In other words, the trade union opposition is manifestly developing in the reformist spirit.

23. It is entirely wrong to affirm that in these recent years — contrary to what has happened in Germany, Czechoslovakia, and other countries — there has not been constituted in France a right-wing grouping in the revolutionary camp. The main point is that, forsaking the revolutionary policy of Communism, the right opposition in France, in conformity with the traditions of the French labor movement, has assumed a trade union character, concealing in this way its political physiognomy. At bottom, the majority of the trade union opposition represents the right wing, just as the Brandler group [18] in Germany, the Czech trade unionists who, after the split, have taken a clearly reformist position, etc.

24. One may seek to object that all the preceding considerations would be correct only on condition that the Communist Party has a correct policy. But this objection is unfounded. The question of the relationships between the party, which represents the proletariat as it should be, and the trade unions, which represent the proletariat as it is, is the most fundamental question of revolutionary Marxism. It would be veritable suicide to spurn the only possible principled reply to this question solely because the Communist Party, under the in-

fluence of objective and subjective reasons of which we have spoken more than once, is now conducting a false policy towards the trade unions, as well as in other fields. A correct policy must be counterposed to a wrong policy. Towards this end, the Left Opposition has been constituted as a faction. If it is considered that the French Communist Party in its entirety is in a wholly irremediable or hopeless state — which we absolutely do not think — another party must be counterposed to it. But the question of the relation of the party to the class does not change one iota by this fact.

The Left Opposition considers that to influence the trade union movement, to help it find its correct orientation, to permeate it with correct slogans, is impossible except through the Communist Party (or a faction for the moment) which, besides its other attributes, is the central ideological laboratory of the working class.

25. The correctly understood task of the Communist Party does not consist solely of gaining influence over the trade unions, such as they are, but in winning, through the trade unions, an influence over the majority of the working class. This is possible only if the methods employed by the party in the trade unions correspond to the nature and the tasks of the latter. The struggle for influence of the party in the trade unions finds its objective verification in the fact that they do or do not thrive, and in the fact that the number of their members increases, as well as in their relations with the broadest masses. If the party buys its influence in the trade unions only at the price of a narrowing down and a factionalizing of the latter — converting them into auxiliaries of the party for momentary aims and preventing them from becoming genuine mass organizations — the relations between the party and the class are wrong. It is not necessary for us to dwell here on the causes for such a situation. We have done it more than once and we do it every day. The changeability of the official Communist policy reflects its adventurist tendency to make itself master of the working class in the briefest time, by means of stage-play, inventions, superficial agitation, etc.

The way out of this situation does not, however, lie in counterposing the trade unions to the party (or to the faction) but in the irreconcilable struggle to change the whole policy of the party as well as that of the trade unions.

26. The Left Opposition must place the questions of the trade union movement in indissoluble connection with the questions of the political struggle of the proletariat. It must give a concrete analysis of the present stage of development of the French labor movement. It must give an evaluation, quantitative as well as qualitative, of the present strike movement and its perspectives in relation to the perspectives of the economic development of France. It is needless to say that it completely rejects the perspective of capitalist stabilization and

pacifism for decades. It proceeds from an estimation of our epoch as a revolutionary one. It springs from the necessity of a timely preparation of the vanguard proletariat in face of the abrupt turns which are not only probable but inevitable. The firmer and more implacable is its action against the supposedly revolutionary rantings of the centrist bureaucracy, against political hysteria which does not take conditions into account, which confuses today with yesterday or with tomorrow, the more firmly and resolutely must it set itself against the elements of the right that take up its criticism and conceal themselves under it in order to introduce their tendencies into revolutionary Marxism.

27. A new definition of boundaries? New polemics? New splits? That will be the lament of the good but tired souls, who would like to transform the Opposition into a calm retreat where one can tranquilly rest from the great tasks, while preserving intact the name of revolutionist "of the left." No! we say to them, to these tired souls: we are certainly not traveling the same road. Truth has never yet been the sum of small errors. A revolutionary organization has never yet been composed of small conservative groups, seeking primarily to distinguish themselves from each other. There are epochs when the revolutionary tendency is reduced to a small minority in the labor movement. But these epochs demand not arrangements between the small groups with mutual hiding of sins but, on the contrary, a doubly implacable struggle for a correct perspective and an education of the cadres in the spirit of genuine Marxism. Victory is possible only in this way.

28. So far as the author of these lines is personally concerned, he must admit that the notion he had of the Monatte group when he was deported from the Soviet Union proved to be too optimistic and, by that fact, false. For many years, the author did not have the possibility of following the activity of this group. He judged it from old memories. The divergences showed themselves in fact not only profounder but even more acute than one might have supposed. The events of recent times have proved beyond a doubt that, without a clear and precise ideological demarcation from the line of syndicalism, the Communist Opposition in France will not go forward. The theses proposed represent by themselves the first step on the road of this demarcation, which is the prelude to the successful struggle against the revolutionary jabberings and the opportunist essence of Cachin, Monmousseau and Company.[19]

October 14, 1929.

The Errors in Principle of Syndicalism

To Serve in the Discussion with Monatte and his Friends

When I arrived in France in October 1914, I found the French socialist and trade union movement in a state of the deepest chauvinist demoralization. In the search for revolutionists, with candle in hand, I made the acquaintance of Monatte and Rosmer.[20] They had not succumbed to chauvinism. It was thus that our friendship began. Monatte considered himself an anarcho-syndicalist; despite that, he was immeasurably closer to me than the French Guesdists,[21] who were playing a pitiful and shameful role. At that time, the Cachins were making themselves familiar with the servants' entrance to the ministries of the Third Republic[22] and the Allied embassies. In 1915, Monatte left the central committee of the CGT, slamming the door behind him. His departure from the trade union center was in essence nothing but a split. At that time, however, Monatte believed—and rightly so—that the fundamental historical tasks of the proletariat stood above unity with chauvinists and lackeys of imperialism. It was in this that Monatte was loyal to the best traditions of revolutionary syndicalism.

Monatte was one of the first friends of the October Revolution. True, unlike Rosmer, he had held aloof for a long time. That was well in keeping with the character of Monatte, as I was later convinced, of standing aside, of waiting, of criticizing. At times this is absolutely unavoidable. But as a *basic* line of conduct, it becomes a kind of sectarianism that has a close affinity to Proudhonism,[23] but nothing in common with Marxism.

When the Socialist Party of France became the Communist Party, I frequently had occasion to discuss with Lenin the onerous heritage the International had received in the person of leaders like Cachin, Frossard and other heroes of the League of the Rights of Man, of the Freemasons, of parliamentarians, careerists, and babblers. One of these conversations—if I am not mistaken I have already published it in the press—follows:

"It would be good," Lenin said to me, "to drive out all these weathercocks, and to draw into the party the revolutionary syndicalists, the militant workers, people who are really devoted to the cause of the working class. And Monatte?"

"Monatte would of course be ten times better than Cachin and those like him," I replied. "But Monatte not only continues to reject parliamentarism but to this day he has not grasped the significance of the party."

Lenin was astonished: "Impossible! Has not grasped the significance of the party after the October Revolution? That's a very disturbing symptom."

I carried on a correspondence with Monatte in which I invited him to Moscow. He was evasive. True to his nature, he preferred in this case too to stand aside and wait. And besides, the Communist Party did not suit him. In that he was right. But instead of helping to transform it, he waited. At the Fourth Congress we succeeded in taking the first step towards cleansing the Communist Party of France of Freemasons, pacifists and office-seekers. Monatte entered the party. But it is not necessary to emphasize the fact that this did not mean to us that he had adopted the Marxian viewpoint; not at all. On March 23, 1923, I wrote in *Pravda:* The entrance of our old friend Monatte into the Communist Party was a great day for us. The revolution needs men of this kind. But it would be wrong to pay for a *rapprochement* with a confusion of ideas." In this article, I criticized the scholasticism of Louzon on the relations among the class, the trade unions, and the party. In particular, I explained that prewar syndicalism had been an embryo of the Communist Party, that this embryo had since become a child, and that, if this child was suffering from measles and rickets, it was necessary to nourish and cure it, but that it would be absurd to imagine that it could be made to return to its mother's womb. I may perhaps be permitted to say in this regard that the arguments of my 1923 article, in caricature, serve to this day as the main weapons against Monatte in the hands of Monmousseau and other anti-Trotskyist warriors.

Monatte joined the party; but he hardly had time to turn about and accustom himself to a house far vaster than his little shop on the *Quai de Jemmapes* [24] when the *coup d'état* in the International burst upon him: Lenin was taken ill, the campaign against "Trotskyism" and the Zinovievist "Bolshevization" began. Monatte could not submit to the careerists who, by leaning on the general staff of the epigones at Moscow and disposing of unlimited resources, carried on by means of intrigue and slander. Monatte was expelled from the party. This episode, important but still only an episode, was of decisive moment in the political development of Monatte. He decided that his brief experience in the party had fully confirmed his anarcho-syndicalist prejudices against the party in general. Monatte then began insistently to retrace his steps towards abandoned positions. He began to seek again the Amiens Charter. [25] To do all that, he had to turn his face to the past. The experiences of the war, of the Russian Revolution, and of the world trade union movement were lost upon him, leaving hardly a trace. Once again Monatte stood aside and waited. What for? A new Amiens Congress. During the last few years I was unfortunately unable to follow the retrogressive evolution of Monatte: the Russian Opposition lived in a blockaded circle.

Out of the whole treasure of the theory and practice of the world struggle of the proletariat, Monatte has extracted but two ideas: *trade union autonomy* and *trade union unity*. He has elevated these two pure principles above sinful reality. It is on trade union autonomy and trade union unity that he has based his newspaper and his Syndicalist League. Unfortunately, these two ideas are hollow and each of them resembles the hole in a ring. Whether the ring be made of iron, silver or gold, Monatte does not care in the least. The ring, you see, always hampers the trade unions' activity. Monatte is interested only in the hole of autonomy.

No less empty is the other sacred principle: *unity*. In its name, Monatte even stood out against the rupture of the Anglo-Russian Committee,[26] even though the General Council of the British trade unions had betrayed the general strike. The fact that Stalin, Bukharin, Cachin, Monmousseau and others supported the bloc with the strikebreakers until the latter kicked them out, does not in the least reduce Monatte's mistake. After my arrival abroad, I made an attempt to explain to the readers of the *Révolution prolétarienne*[27] the criminal character of this bloc, the consequences of which are still being felt by the workers' movement. Monatte did not want to publish my article. And how could it have been otherwise, since I had made an assault upon the sacred trade union unity, which solves all questions and reconciles all contradictions?

When strikers encounter a group of strikebreakers in their path, they throw them out of their midst without sparing blows. If the strikebreakers are union men, they throw them out immediately, without worrying about the sacred principle of trade union unity. Monatte surely has no objections to this. But the matter is entirely different when it is a question of the trade union bureaucracy and its leaders. The General Council is not composed of starving and backward strikebreakers; no, they are well-fed and experienced traitors, who found it necessary at a given moment to stand at the head of the general strike in order to decapitate it all the more quickly and surely. They worked hand in hand with the government, the bosses, and the church. It would seem that the leaders of the Russian trade unions, who were in a political bloc with the General Council, should have immediately, openly and relentlessly broken with it at that very moment, in full view of the masses deceived and betrayed by it. But Monatte rises up fiercely: it is forbidden to disturb trade union unity. In an astonishing manner, he forgets that he himself upset this unity in 1915 by leaving the chauvinist General Council of the *Confédération Générale du Travail*.

It must be said outright: between the Monatte of 1915 and the Monatte of 1929, there is an abyss. To Monatte it seems that he is remaining entirely faithful to himself. Formally, this is true, up to a certain point. Monatte repeats a few old formulas, but he ignores entirely the experiences of the last fifteen years, richer in lessons than all the preceding history of humanity. In the attempt to return to his former positions, Monatte fails to notice that they disappeared a long time ago. No matter what question is raised, Monatte looks backward. This may be seen most clearly in the question of the party and the state.

Some time ago, Monatte accused me of underrating the "dangers" of state power (*Révolution prolétarienne,* No. 79, May 1, 1929, page 2). This reproach is not a new one; it has its origin in the struggle of Bakunin against Marx and it shows a false, contradictory, and essentially nonproletarian conception of the state.

With the exception of one country, state power throughout the world is in the hands of the bourgeoisie. *It is in this, and only in this, that, from the point of view of the proletariat, the danger of state power lies.* The proletariat's historical task is to wrest this most powerful instrument of oppression from the hands of the bourgeoisie. The Communists do not deny the difficulties, the dangers that are connected with the dictatorship of the proletariat. But can this lessen by one iota the necessity to seize power? If the whole proletariat were carried by an irresistible force to the conquest of power, or if it had already conquered it, one could, strictly speaking, understand this or that warning of the syndicalists. Lenin, as is known, warned in his testament [28] against the abuse of revolutionary power. The struggle against the distortions of the dictatorship of the proletariat has been conducted by the Opposition since its inception and without the need of borrowing from the arsenal of anarchism.

But in the bourgeois countries, the misfortune lies in the fact that the overwhelming majority of the proletariat does not understand as it should the dangers of the *bourgeois* state. By the manner in which they treat the question, the syndicalists, unwittingly of course, contribute to the passive conciliation of the workers with the capitalist state. When the syndicalists keep drumming into the workers, who are oppressed by the bourgeois state, their warnings about the dangers of a proletarian state, they play a purely reactionary role. The bourgeois will readily repeat to the workers: "Do not touch the state because it is a snare full of dangers to you." The Communist will say to the workers: "The difficulties and dangers with which the proletariat is confronted the day after the conquest of power — we will learn to overcome them on the basis of experience. But at the present time, the most menacing dangers lie in the fact that our class enemy holds the reins of power in its hands and directs it against us."

In contemporary society, there are only two classes capable of holding power in their hands: the capitalist bourgeoisie and the revolutionary proletariat. The petty bourgeoisie long ago lost the economic possibility of directing the destinies of modern society. Now and then, in fits of desperation, it rises for the conquest of power, even with arms in hand, as has happened in Italy, in Poland and other countries.

But the fascist insurrections only end in this result: the new power becomes the instrument of finance capital under an even more naked and brutal form. That is why the most representative ideologists of the petty bourgeoisie are afraid of state power as such. The petty bourgeoisie fears power when it is in the hands of the big bourgeoisie, because the latter strangles and ruins it. The petty bourgeoisie also fears power when it is in the hands of the proletariat, for the latter undermines all the conditions of its habitual existence. Finally, it fears power when it falls into its own hands because it must inevitably pass out of its impotent hands into those of finance capital or the proletariat. The anarchists do not see the revolutionary problems of state power, its historical role, and see only the "dangers" of state power. The anti-state anarchists are consequently the most logical and, for that reason, the most hopeless representatives of the petty bourgeoisie in its historical blind alley.

Yes, the dangers of state power exist under the regime of the dictatorship of the proletariat as well, but the substance of these dangers consists of the fact that power can actually return to the hands of the bourgeoisie. The best known and most obvious state danger is *bureaucratism*. But what is its essence? If the enlightened workers' bureaucracy could lead society to socialism, that is, to the liquidation of the state, we would be reconciled to such a bureaucracy. But it has an entirely opposite *character*: by separating itself from the proletariat, by raising itself above it, the bureaucracy falls under the influence of the petty bourgeois classes and can by that very fact facilitate the return of power into the hands of the bourgeoisie. In other words, the state dangers for the workers under the dictatorship of the proletariat are, in the final analysis, nothing but the danger of restoring the power to the bourgeoisie.

The question of the *source* of this bureaucratic danger is no less important. It would be radically wrong to think, to imagine, that bureaucratism rises exclusively from the fact of the conquest of power by the proletariat. No, that is not the case. In the capitalist states, the most monstrous forms of bureaucratism are to be observed precisely in the trade unions. It is enough to look at America, England and Germany. Amsterdam [29] is the most powerful international organization of the trade union bureaucracy. It is thanks to it that the whole structure of capitalism now stands upright, above all in Europe and especially in England. If there were not a bureaucracy of the trade unions, then the police, the army, the courts, the lords, the monarchy would appear before the proletarian masses as nothing but pitiful and ridiculous playthings. The bureaucracy of the trade unions is the backbone of British imperialism. It is by means of this bureaucracy that the bourgeoisie exists, not only in the metropolis, but in India, in Egypt, and in the other colonies. One would have to be completely blind to say to the English workers: "Be on guard against the conquest of power and always remember that your trade unions are the antidote to the dangers of the state." The Marxist will say to the English workers: "The trade union bureaucracy is the chief instrument for your oppression by the bourgeois state. Power must be wrested from the hands of the bourgeoisie, and for that its principal agent, the trade union bureaucracy, must be overthrown." Parenthetically, it is especially for this reason that the bloc of Stalin with the strike-breakers was so criminal.

From the example of England, one sees very clearly how absurd it is to counterpose, as if it were a question of two different principles, the trade union organization and the state organization. In England, more than anywhere else, the state rests upon the back of the working class which constitutes the overwhelming majority of the population of the country. The mechanism is such that the bureaucracy is based *directly* on the workers, and the state indirectly, *through the intermediary* of the trade union bureaucracy.

Up to now, we have not mentioned the Labour Party, which in England, the classic country of trade unions, is only a political transposition of the same trade union bureaucracy. The same leaders guide the trade unions, betray the general strike, lead the electoral campaign and later on sit in the ministries. The Labour Party and the trade unions — these are not two principles, they are only a technical division of labor. Together they are the fundamental support of the domination of the English bourgeoisie. The latter cannot be overthrown without overthrowing the Labourite bureaucracy. And that cannot be attained by counterposing the trade union as such to the state as such, but only by the active opposition of the Communist Party to the Labourite bureaucracy in all fields of social life: in the trade unions, in strikes, in the electoral campaign, in parliament, and in power. The principal task of a real party of the proletariat consists of putting itself at the head of the working masses, organized in trade unions and unorganized, to wrest power from the bourgeoisie and to strike a deathblow to the "dangers of statism."

Constantinople, October 21, 1929

Monatte Crosses the Rubicon [30]

It is now ridiculous and out of place to speak of joint action with the Syndicalist League or the Committee for the Independence of Trade Unionism. Monatte has crossed the Rubicon. He has lined up with Dumoulin against Communism, against the October Revolution, against the proletarian revolution in general. For Dumoulin belongs to the camp of the especially dangerous and perfidious enemies of the proletarian revolution. He has demonstrated in action, in the most repugnant manner. For a long time he has prowled around the left wing only to rally at the decisive moment to Jouhaux, that is, to the most servile and most corrupt agent of capital. The task of the honest revolutionist, above all in France where unpunished betrayals are innumerable, consists of reminding the workers of the experiences of the past, of tempering the youth in intransigence, of recounting tirelessly the history of the betrayal of the Second International and of French syndicalism, of unmasking the shameful role played not only by Jouhaux and Company, but above all by the French syndicalists of the "left," like Merrheim and Dumoulin. Whoever does not carry out this elementary task towards the new generation deprives himself forever of the right to revolutionary confidence. Can one, for instance, preserve a shadow of esteem for the toothless French anarchists when they again play up as an "antimilitarist" the old buffoon Sébastian Faure who trafficked with pacifist phrases in peacetime and flung himself into the arms of Malvy, [31] that is, of the French Bourse, [32] at the beginning of the war? Whoever seeks to drape these facts in the toga of oblivion, who grants amnesty to political traitors, can only be considered by us an incorrigible enemy.

Monatte has crossed the Rubicon. From the uncertain ally, he has become first the hesitant foe in order to become, later on, the direct enemy. We must say this to the workers clearly, aloud, and unsparingly.

To simple people and also to some knaves who put on a simple air, our judgment may appear exaggerated and "unjust." For Monatte is uniting with Dumoulin *solely* for the reestablishment of the unity of the "trade union" movement! Solely! The trade unions, you see, are not a party nor a "sect." The trade unions, you see, must embrace the whole working class, all its tendencies; one can therefore work in the trade union field by Dumoulin's side without taking responsibility either for his past or for his future. Reflections of this sort constitute a chain of those cheap sophisms with which the French syndicalists and socialists love to juggle when they want to cover up a somewhat odorous job.

If there existed in France united trade unions, the revolutionists would obviously not have left the organization because of the presence of traitors, turncoats and licensed agents of imperialism. The revolutionists would not have taken upon themselves the initiative for the split. But in joining or in remaining in these trade unions, they would have directed all their efforts *to unmasking the traitors before the masses as traitors,* in order to discredit them on the basis of the experience of the masses, to isolate them, to deprive them of the confidence they enjoy, and in the end, to help the masses run them out. That alone can justify the participation of revolutionists in the reformist trade unions.

But Monatte does not at all work side by side with Dumoulin within the trade unions, as the Bolsheviks frequently had to with the Mensheviks while conducting a systematic struggle against them. No, *Monatte has united with Dumoulin as an ally* on a common platform, creating with him a political faction or a "sect" expressing itself in the language of French syndicalism in order later on to lead a political crusade for the conquest of the trade union movement. Monatte does not fight against the traitors on the trade union field; on the contrary, he has associated himself with Dumoulin and takes him under his wing, presenting himself to the masses as Dumoulin's tutor. Monatte says to the workers that one can go hand in hand with Dumoulin against the Communists, against the Red International of Labor Unions, against the October Revolution, and consequently, against the proletarian revolution in general. This is the unvarnished truth which we must speak aloud to the workers.

When we once defined Monatte as a *centrist slipping towards the right,* Chambelland [33] sought to transform this entirely correct scientific definition into a feuilleton joke and even to throw the centrist designation back at us, just as a soccer player returns the ball by hitting it with his head. Alas, the head sometimes suffers for it! Yes, Monatte was a centrist, and in his centrism were contained all the elements of his manifest opportunism of today.

Apropos of the execution of the Indochinese revolutionists in the spring of this year, [34] Monatte developed the following plan of action, in an indirect manner:

"I do not understand why, in such circumstances, the parties and organizations disposing of the necessary means do not send deputies and journalists to investigate on the very spot. Out of the dozen deputies of the Communist Party, and out of the hundred of the Socialist Party, could they not select an investigation commission which would be charged with the elements of a campaign capable of making the colonialists retreat and of saving the condemned?" (*Révolution prolétarienne,* No. 104.)

With the imperious reproaches of a school monitor, Monatte gave the Communists and the social democrats advice on the manner of fighting against the "colonialists." The social-patriots and the Communists, for him, were six months ago people *of the same camp* who had only to follow Monatte's advice in order to carry out a correct policy. For Monatte there did not even exist the question of knowing in what way the social-patriots can fight against the "colonialists" when they are the partisans and the practical executors of the colonial policy. For can colonies, that is, nations, tribes, races, be governed without shooting down the rebels, the revolutionists who seek to liberate themselves from the repulsive colonial yoke? Zyromsky [35] and his ilk are not opposed to presenting upon every propitious occasion a drawing-room protest against colonial "bestiality"; but that does not prevent them from belonging to the social-colonialist party which harnessed the French proletariat to a chauvinistic course during the war, one of whose principal aims was to preserve and extend the colonies to the profit of the French bourgeoisie. Monatte has forgotten all this. He reasoned as if there had not been, after this, great revolutionary events in a number of Western and Oriental countries, as if different tendencies had not been revised in action and made clear by experience. Six months ago, Monatte pretended to start all over again. And during this time, history again made game of him. MacDonald,[36] the coreligionist of the French syndicalists, to whom Louzon recently gave some incomparable advice, sends to India not liberating commissions of investigation but armed forces, and comes to grips with the Hindus in a more repulsive manner than would any Curzon.[37] And all the scoundrels of British trade unionism approve this butcher's work. Is this by chance?

Instead of turning away, under the influence of the new lesson, from hypocritical "neutrality" and "independence," Monatte, on the contrary, has taken a new step, this time a decisive one, into the arms of the French MacDonalds and Thomases.[38] We have nothing more to discuss with Monatte.

The bloc of the "independent" syndicalists with the avowed agents of the bourgeoisie has great symptomatic significance. In the eyes of philistines, things seem as though the representatives of both camps had taken a step towards each other in the name of unity, of the cessation of the fratricidal struggle, and other sweet phrases. There can be nothing more disgusting, more false, than this phraseology. In reality the meaning of the bloc is entirely different.

In the various circles of the labor bureaucracy and also in part in circles of the workers themselves, Monatte represents those elements who sought to approach the revolution but who lost hope in it through the experience of the last ten or twelve years. Don't you see that it develops by such complicated and perplexing roads that it leads to internal conflicts, to ever new splits, and after a step forward it takes a half step and sometimes a full step backward? The years of bourgeois stabilization, the years of the ebbing of the revolutionary tide, have heaped up despair, fatigue, and opportunist moods in a certain part of the working class. All these sentiments have only now matured in the Monatte group and have driven it to pass definitively from one camp to the other. On the way, Monatte met with Louis Sellier,[39] who had his own reasons for turning his back, covered with municipal honors, to the revolution. Monatte and Sellier have quit together. To their meeting, there came no less a one than Dumoulin. This means that at the moment when Monatte shifted from left to right, Dumoulin judged it opportune to shift from right to left. How is this to be explained? It is because Monatte, as an empiricist — and centrists are always empiricists, otherwise they would not be centrists — has expressed his sentiments on the stabilization period at a moment when this period *has begun to be transformed into another, much less tranquil and much less stable.*

The world crisis has taken on gigantic dimensions and for the moment it is becoming deeper. Nobody can predict where it will stop or what political consequences it will bring in its train. The situation in Germany is extremely strained. The German elections produced acute elements of disturbance, not only in internal relations but also in international relations, showing again on what foundation the edifice of Versailles [40] rests. The economic crisis has inundated the frontiers of France, and we already see there, after a long interlude, the beginnings of unemployment. During the years of relative prosperity, the French workers suffered from the policy of the confederal bureaucracy. During the years of crisis, they can remind it of its betrayals and its crimes. Jouhaux cannot but be uneasy. He necessarily requires a left wing, perhaps more necessarily than Blum. What purpose then does Dumoulin serve? Obviously it must not be thought that everything is arranged like the notes of a piano and has been formulated in a conversation. That is not necessary. All these people know each other, they know what they are capable of and especially the limits to which one of them can go to the left, with impunity for himself and his bosses. (The fact that the confederal bureaucracy preserves a watchful and critical attitude towards Dumoulin, sometimes even with a nuance of hostility, in no way invalidates what is said above. The reformists must take their measures of precaution and keep an eye upon Dumoulin so that he does not let himself get carried away by the work with which the reformists have charged him and go beyond the limits marked out.)

Dumoulin takes his place in the line of march as the left wing of Jouhaux at the very moment when Monatte, who has shifted constantly to the right, has decided to cross the Rubicon. Dumoulin must reestablish his reputation at least a little — with the aid of Monatte and at his expense. Jouhaux can have no objection when his own Dumoulin compromises Monatte. In this way, everything is in order: Monatte has broken with the left camp at the moment when the confederal bureaucracy has felt the necessity of covering up its uncovered left flank.

We are analyzing personal shifts not for Monatte, who was once our friend, and certainly not for Dumoulin, whom we long ago judged as an irreconcilable enemy. What interests us is the *symptomatic* significance of these personal regroupings, which reflect far more profound processes in the working masses themselves.

This radicalization which the clamorers proclaimed two years ago is indisputably approaching today. The economic crisis has arrived in France — after a delay, it is true; it is not impossible that it will unfold in a mild manner compared with Germany. Experience alone can establish this. But it is indisputable that the balanced state of passivity in which the French working class existed in the years of the so-called "radicalization" will give way in a very brief time to a growing activity and a spirit of militancy. It is towards this new period that the revolutionists must turn.

On the threshold of the new period, Monatte gathers up the fatigued, the disillusioned, the exhausted, and makes them pass into the camp of Jouhaux. So much the worse for Monatte, so much the better for the revolution!

The period opening before us will not be a period of the growth of the false neutrality of the trade unions but, on the contrary, the period of the reinforcement of the Communist positions in the labor movement. Great tasks present themselves to the Left Opposition. With sure successes awaiting it, what must it do to gain them? Nothing but *remain faithful to itself.* But, on this point, next time.

Prinkipo, December 15, 1930.

The Mistakes of Rightist Elements Of the Communist League On the Trade Union Question

Some Preliminary Remarks

1. If the theoretical structure of the political economy of Marxism rests entirely upon the conception of *value* as materialized labor, the revolutionary policy of Marxism rests upon the conception of the *party* as the vanguard of the proletariat.

Whatever may be the social sources and political causes of opportunistic mistakes and deviations, they are always reduced ideologically to an erroneous understanding of the revolutionary party, of its relation to other proletarian organizations and to the class as a whole.

2. The conception of the party as the proletarian vanguard presupposes its full and unconditional independence from all other organizations. The various agreements (blocs, coalitions, compromises) with other organizations, unavoidable in the course of the class struggle, are permissible only on the condition that the party always turns its own face towards the class, always marches under its own banner, acts in its own name, and clearly explains to the masses the aims and limits within which it concludes the given agreement.

3. At the basis of all the oscillations and all the errors of the Comin-

tern leadership, we find the wrong understanding of the nature of the party and its tasks. The Stalinist theory of a "two-class party" contradicts the ABC of Marxism. The fact that the official Communist International has tolerated this theory for a number of years, and to this day has not yet condemned it with the necessary firmness, is the most unmistakable sign of the falsity of its official doctrine.

4. The fundamental crime of the centrist bureaucracy in the USSR is its false position regarding the party. The Stalinist faction seeks to include administratively in the ranks of the party the whole working class. The party ceases to be the vanguard, that is, the voluntary selection of the most advanced, the most conscious, the most devoted, and the most active workers. The party is fused with the class as it is and loses its power of resistance to the bureaucratic apparatus. On the other hand, the Brandlerites and the other hangers-on of the centrist bureaucracy justify the Stalinist party regime by the philistine reference to the "lack of culture" of the Russian proletariat, thus identifying the party and the class, that is, liquidating the party in theory as Stalin liquidates it in practice.

5. The basis of the disastrous policy of the Comintern in China was the renunciation of the independence of the party. Practical agreements with the Kuomintang [41] were unavoidable in a certain period. The entrance of the Communist Party into the Kuomintang was a fatal error. The development of this mistake was transformed into one of the greatest crimes in history. The Chinese Communist Party was created only in order to transfer its authority to the Kuomintang. From the vanguard of the proletariat, it was transformed into the tail of the bourgeoisie.

6. The disastrous experiment with the Anglo-Russian Committee was based entirely upon trampling under foot the independence of the British Communist Party. In order that the Soviet trade unions might maintain the bloc with the strikebreakers of the General Council (allegedly in the state interests of the USSR!), the British Communist Party had to be deprived of all independence. This was obtained by the actual dissolution of the party into the so-called Minority Movement, that is, the leftist opposition inside the trade unions.

7. The experience of the Anglo-Russian Committee was unfortunately the least understood and grasped even in the Left Opposition groups. The demands for a break with the strikebreakers appeared even to some within our ranks as sectarianism. Especially with Monatte, the original sin which led him into the arms of Dumoulin was most clearly manifested in the question of the Anglo-Russian Committee. Yet, this question has a gigantic importance: without a clear understanding of what happened in England in 1925-26, neither Communism as a whole nor the Left Opposition in particular will be able to make its way to a broad road.

8. Stalin, Bukharin, Zinoviev — in this question they were all in soli-

darity, at least initially — sought to replace the weak British Communist Party by a "broader current," which had at its head, to be sure, not members of the party, but "friends," almost-Communists, at any rate fine fellows and good acquaintances. The fine fellows, the "solid leaders," did not, of course, want to submit themselves to the leadership of a small, weak Communist Party. That was their full right; the party cannot force anybody to submit himself to it. The agreements between the Communists and the "lefts" (Purcell, Hicks, Cook) [42] on the basis of the partial tasks of the trade union movement were, of course, quite possible and in certain cases essential. But on one condition: the Communist Party had to preserve its complete independence, even within the trade unions, act in its own name in all the questions of principle, criticize its "left" allies whenever necessary, and in this way win the confidence of the masses step by step.

This only possible road, however, appeared too long and uncertain to the bureaucrats of the CI. They considered that by means of personal influence upon Purcell, Hicks, Cook and the others (conversations behind the scenes, correspondence, banquets, friendly backslapping, gentle exhortations), they would gradually and imperceptibly draw the leftist opposition ("the broad current") into the bed of the Communist International. To guarantee such a success with greater security, the dear friends (Purcell, Hicks and Cook) were not to be vexed or exasperated or displeased by petty chicanery, by inopportune criticism, by sectarian intransigence, and so forth. But since one of the tasks of the Communist Party consists precisely of upsetting the peace of and alarming all centrists and semicentrists, a radical measure had to be resorted to by actually subordinating the CP to the Minority Movement. On the trade union field appeared only the leaders of this movement. The British Communist Party had practically ceased to exist for the masses.

9. What did the Russian Left Opposition demand in this question? In the first place, to reestablish the complete independence of the British Communist Party in relation to the trade unions. We affirmed that it is only under the influence of the independent slogans of the party and of its open criticism that the Minority Movement could take form, appreciate its tasks more precisely, change its leaders, fortify itself in the trade unions while consolidating the position of Communism.

What did Stalin, Bukharin, Losovsky and Company [43] reply to our criticism? "You want to push the British Communist Party onto the road of sectarianism. You want to drive Purcell, Hicks and Cook into the enemy's camp. You want to break with the Minority Movement."

What did the Left Opposition rejoin? "If Purcell and Hicks break with us, not because we demand of them that they transform themselves immediately into Communists — nobody demands that! — but because we ourselves want to remain Communists, this means that

Purcell and Company are not friends but masked enemies. The quicker they show their real nature, the better for the masses. We do not at all want to break with the Minority Movement. On the contrary, we must give the greatest attention to this movement. The smallest step forward with the masses or with a part of the masses is worth more than a dozen abstract programs of circles of intellectuals, but the attention devoted to the masses has nothing in common with capitulation before their temporary leaders and semileaders. The masses need a correct orientation and correct slogans. This excludes all theoretical conciliation and all protection of confusionists who exploit the backwardness of the masses."

10. What were the results of the British experiment of Stalin? The Minority Movement, embracing almost a million workers, seemed very promising, but it bore the germs of destruction within itself. The masses knew as the leaders of the movement only Purcell, Hicks, and Cook, whom, moreover, Moscow vouched for. These "left" friends, in the first serious test, shamefully betrayed the proletariat. The revolutionary workers were thrown into confusion, sank into apathy, and naturally extended their disappointment to the CP itself, which had only been the passive part of this whole mechanism of betrayal and perfidy. The Minority Movement was reduced to zero; the Communist Party returned to the existence of a negligible sect. In this way, thanks to a radically false conception of the party, the greatest movement of the English proletariat, which led to the general strike, not only did not shake the apparatus of the reactionary bureaucracy, but, on the contrary, reinforced it and compromised Communism in Great Britain for a long time.

11. One of the psychological sources of opportunism is a superficial impatience, a lack of confidence in the gradual growth of the party's influence, the desire to win the masses by organizational maneuvers or personal diplomacy. Out of this springs the policy of combinations behind the scenes, the policy of silence, of hushing up, of self-renunciation, of adaptation to the ideas and slogans of others; and finally, the complete passage to the positions of opportunism. The subordination of the CP to the Kuomintang in China, the creation of workers' and peasants' parties in India, the subordination of the British party to the Minority Movement, etc., etc. — in all these phenomena we see the same method of bureaucratic combinationism which commences with a superficial revolutionary impatience and finishes with opportunist treason. *

------

*The leading comrades in the United States inform us that in the American League certain comrades—to be sure, only individual ones (in the literal sense of the word)—speak for the bloc with the Lovestoneites [44] in the name of "mass work." It is hard to imagine a more ridiculous, a more inept, a more sterile project than this. Do these people know at least a little of the history of the Bolshevik Party? Have they read the works of Lenin? Do they know the correspondence of Marx

That is precisely why we have constantly insisted in these last few years upon the enormous educational importance of examples of the Comintern's strategy cited above. They should be studied and checked all over again at each fresh experience, not only in order to condemn the historical mistakes and crimes after the fact, but to learn to discern similar errors in a new situation at their very inception and consequently while they can still be corrected.

12. It must be said directly: the mistakes of some French Oppositionists, members of the League, on the trade union question reveal striking traits of resemblance with the lamentable British experiment. Only, the scale of the errors in France is as yet much smaller, and they have not developed on the basis of a mass movement. This permits certain comrades to overlook these mistakes or to underestimate their importance in principle. Nevertheless, should the League similarly permit its trade union work to be carried on in the future by the methods formulated by the majority of the old leadership, the ideas and the banner of the Left Opposition would be compromised in France for a long time to come.

It would have been criminal to close one's eyes to this. Since there has been no success in rectifying these errors in their initial stage by means of private advice and warnings, then there only remains to name these errors and their authors openly in order to rectify the policy through collective efforts.

13. Beginning with April 1930, the League, in effect, gave up independent work in the trade unions for the benefit of the Unitary Opposition which, on its part, strives to have its own platform, its leadership, its policy. Within these limits we have a striking analogy with the experiment of the Minority Movement in England. It must, however, be said that in the French circumstances there are certain features which, from the very beginning, render this experiment still more dangerous. In England, the Minority Movement as a whole was *more to the left* than the official leadership of the trade unions.

Can this be said of the Unitary Opposition? No. In the ranks of the latter there are elements who are obviously tending towards the Right Opposition, that is, towards reformism. Their specific weight is not as yet clear to us.

The principal force of the Unitary Opposition is the Teachers' Federation. In France, the teachers have always played a serious role in socialism, in syndicalism, and in Communism. Among the teachers, we shall no doubt find many friends. Nevertheless, the federation as a whole is not a proletarian federation. Because of its social composition, the Teachers' Federation can furnish very good agitators, jour-

---

and Engels? Or has all the history of the revolutionary movement passed them by without leaving a trace? Fortunately, the overwhelming majority of the American League has nothing in common with such ideas. — L. T.

nalists, and individual revolutionists, but it cannot become the basis of a trade union movement. All its documents bespeak an insufficient clarity of political thought. The Marseilles congress of the federation demonstrated that its members oscillate in a triangle between the official course, the Left Opposition, and the Right Opposition. We would render the worst service to the members of the federation, as well as to the whole proletarian movement, if we were to cover up their mistakes, their vacillations, their lack of precision. Unfortunately, up to a few days ago this was the policy of the editorial board of *La Vérité*[45]— a policy of silence — and this was not by chance.

14. Then you want to break with the Unitary Opposition? Whoever poses the question this way says by this alone that the Communists, *as Communists*, cannot participate in the work of the Unitary Opposition. But if this were the case, it would signify quite simply that the Unitary Opposition is an organization of the masked enemies of Communism. Happily, this is not so. The UO as a whole is neither a Communist nor an anti-Communist organization, because it is *heterogeneous*. We are obliged to take this heterogeneity into account in our practical activity. We can and must display the greatest attention towards groups and even towards individuals who are developing towards Marxism. But all this on one condition: that when we appear before the workers in the trade unions, we act in the name of the Communist League without admitting any censorship of our acts except the control of the League itself (or the whole party after the reestablishment of the unity of the Communist ranks).

15. In the ranks of the Unitary Opposition there are indisputably elements who sympathize strongly with the Left Opposition without being members of the League; they must be brought together under our banner. There are indefinite elements who strive with all their strength to remain in this position, transforming it into a "platform." With these elements, we can have tactical agreements on a definite basis, preserving full freedom of mutual criticism. Finally, in the ranks of the UO there are also, indisputably, alien elements, who strayed there accidentally, or who penetrated it as recruiting agents of reformism. They make use of obscurity in order to bring about the UO's decomposition. The sooner they are unmasked and eliminated, the better it will be for the cause.

16. But aren't we for collaboration with all workers in the trade unions, regardless of their political and philosophical views? Certainly, but the UO is not a trade union organization; it is a political faction having as its task to influence the trade union movement. Let us leave it to Monatte and his friends the POPists [46] to act under a mask. Revolutionists act openly before the workers. In the UO we can work only with those who go side by side with us, in the same direction, even though not to the end of our road.

17. Certain comrades insist above all that the Communists must

fight for their influence on the trade unions by means of ideas and not by mechanical means. This thought, which may seem incontestable, is frequently converted into an empty commonplace. The centrist bureaucracy also declares quite frequently, and quite sincerely, that its task is to influence by ideas and not to exercise a mechanical pressure.

The whole question, in the last analysis, is reduced to the political and economic orientation, to the slogans and the program of action. If the orientation is right, if the slogans correspond to the needs of the moment, then the masses in the trade unions experience no "constraint." On the contrary, if the orientation is wrong, if the policy of revolutionary ascent is proclaimed at the moment of political ebb, and conversely, then the mass inevitably takes this as a mechanical pressure upon it. The question consequently is reduced to whether the theoretical premises of the Left Opposition are sufficiently serious and profound, if its cadres are sufficiently educated to evaluate the situation correctly and to advance the corresponding slogans. All this must be tested in practice. It is therefore all the more impermissible for us to pass over in silence or to underestimate the sins and the mistakes of our temporary allies as well as of ourselves.

18. Certain members of the League, incredible as it may seem, protest against the intention of somebody or other to subordinate the UO to the League.

Without realizing it, they base themselves on the same wretched argument that Monatte uses against Communism as a whole. In practice, it means that some comrades working in the trade unions want full independence from the League *for themselves*; they think that by their maneuvers, admonitions, and their personal tact they will achieve results that the League cannot attain by collective work. Other comrades, who would like a similar independence for themselves in the press, welcome these tendencies. The question arises: Why did these comrades join the League if they have no confidence in it?

19. How do matters really stand in regard to the "subordination" of the Unitary Opposition? The very question is false. Only its own members are subordinated to the League. As long as the majority of the Unitary Opposition is not in the League, it is a question only of persuasion, compromise, or bloc, but certainly not subordination. In fact, the opponents of the so-called subordination of the Unitary Opposition to the League are demanding the effective subordination of the League to the UO. This was precisely the situation until today. In its trade union work, i. e., in its most important work, the League is subordinated to the Unitary Opposition, for whose benefit it has renounced all independence. Marxists cannot and must not tolerate such a policy — not even for one more day.

20. Certain leading comrades, who obstinately conducted a policy of capitulation up to yesterday, declare today that they are "com-

pletely in agreement" on the necessity of transforming the UO into a bloc. In reality, they want to content themselves with a change of name. The quicker they "agree" with the Marxist criticism, the more they conduct, in actuality, a struggle for everything to remain as before. They simply want to utilize the phraseology of the Marxist criticism in order to cover up the old policy. These methods are not new, but time does not render them more attractive. A revolutionary organization would be corrupted for a long time, if not forever, by the poison of duplicity and falsehood if it permitted an opportunist policy to mask itself with revolutionary phraseology. Let us firmly hope that the League will not permit this.

Prinkipo, January 4, 1931

PART II: PROBLEMS OF UNION STRATEGY AND TACTICS

Preface
by Farrell Dobbs

As a Marxist, Trotsky of course was deeply concerned with all the problems relating to the revolutionary mobilization of the working class, and he followed with interest changes in the trade unions of various countries and the problems of strategy and tactics that these changes presented for revolutionists. In fact he was working on such questions at the time of his death in 1940 ("Trade Unions in the Epoch of Imperialist Decay"). In the second part of the present collection are included that uncompleted article and five others written during the nineteen-thirties.

The first article is about "The Question of Trade Union Unity" as it presented itself to the French Left Oppositionists in 1931 when the unions were divided into two rival labor federations. But Trotsky's treatment of this recurring problem transcends the particular situation which led him to write it, and offers guidelines for handling it even today.

"We make no fetish of trade union unity," he wrote. ". . . It is not a question for us of a panacea." But at the same time, he stressed, "A sure majority in a narrow and isolated trade union confederation, rather than oppositional work in a broad and real mass organization, can be preferred only by sectarians or officials but not by proletarian revolutionists." He did not advocate trade union unity at all times and under all conditions, but he pointed out its advantages under most conditions for the working class as a whole and for the revolutionists in particular.

The second article, here entitled "The Unions in Britain," was written in 1933 after Hitler's coming to power had revealed the bankruptcy of the Communist International. The Left Opposition had decided to discontinue its efforts to reform the Comintern and its parties and to work for the creation of a new international. In line with this, the Left Opposition participated in an international conference of left socialist and independent communist organizations held in Paris August 27-28, 1933, where it introduced a resolution advocating a new international. One of the centrist organizations at the conference, the Independent Labour Party of Great Britain, took an intermediate position on this question because it was still suffering from illusions about the possibility of reforming the Comintern—illusions that were partly the result of ignorance about the history of Stalinism.

In this article, written shortly after the Paris conference, Trotsky undertook the task of educating the members of the ILP, not only about the disastrous policies of the Stalinists in the union sphere in England and elsewhere, but also about the role of genuine revolutionists in combating the union bureaucracy. Among other questions he deals here with one that has still not died: Is it not possible to skip over the trade-union stage?

The third article consists of excerpts from letters in 1936, 7 and 8 criticizing the RSAP (Revolutionary Socialist Workers Party) of Holland, which had adhered to the movement for a new international at the Paris conference in 1933, but which developed a number of serious differences in the following years and withdrew from the movement before the Fourth International was founded in 1938.

The differences covered a broad range of questions—the civil war in Spain, the nature and internal life of the Fourth International, etc. But they also concerned the RSAP's union policy, which was concentrated on a small independent grouping, the Nationaal Arbeids Secretariaat (NAS—National Workers Secretariat), in which the RSAP leader, Henricus Sneevliet, played a leading role, but which remained outside of the mainstream of the Dutch labor movement.

The fourth article is taken from the main document adopted at the founding conference of the Fourth International (The Death Agony of Capitalism and the Tasks of the Fourth International). It repeats the need for revolutionists to work inside the existing unions and condemns "sectarian attempts to build or preserve small 'revolutionary' unions" as "the renouncing of the struggle for leadership of the working class." But it also rejects "trade union fetishism, equally characteristic of trade unionists and syndicalists," advocating a struggle not only to replace the conservative union bureaucracy, but also to create wherever possible independent militant organizations better suited to mass anti-capitalist struggle; and if necessary, "not flinching even in the face of a direct break with the conservative apparatus of the trade unions. If it be criminal to turn one's back on mass organizations for the sake of fostering sectarian fictions, it is no less so to passively tolerate subordination of the revolutionary mass movement to the control of openly reactionary or disguised conservative ('progressive') bureaucratic cliques. Trade unions are not ends in themselves; they are but means along the road to proletarian revolution."

The fifth article is the product of a conversation Trotsky had with a CIO organizer in Mexico in September, 1938, shortly after the founding of the Fourth International.

The final article, which is must reading for every Marxist whether or not he is active in the unions, is one of the most brilliant and prophetic Trotsky ever wrote. Far-ranging, pointing to the conditions that were common to unions all over the world at the start of World War II, it penetrates to the central question of unionism in our time: the need for "complete and unconditional independence of the trade unions in relation to the capitalist state." It is indeed a pity that

Trotsky did not live to complete this article, but there is more food for thought (and action) in this short unfinished piece than will be found in any book by anyone else on the union question.

Other writings and discussions by Trotsky on union problems, especially American problems, will be found in *The Transitional Program for Socialist Revolution,* published by Pathfinder Press.

* * *

"The Question of Trade Union Unity" appeared in the *Militant,* May 15, 1931. "The Unions in Britain" is part of an article that appeared under the title "The ILP and the New International" in the *Militant,* September 30, 1933. The complete article is in *Writings of Leon Trotsky (1933-34).* "Letters on the Dutch Union Situation" are extracts from letters that appeared in the *Internal Bulletin* of the Socialist Workers Party, 1938, No. 5. "Trade Unions in the Transitional Epoch" is taken from the resolution "The Death Agony of Capitalism and the Tasks of the Fourth International." Known as the Transitional Program, it was adopted by the founding conference of the Fourth International in 1938. The complete text is in *The Transitional Program for Socialist Revolution.* "Discussion With a CIO Organizer," translated by George Saunders, appeared in the Russian *Bulletin of the Opposition* No. 71, November 1938. "Trade Unions in the Epoch of Imperialist Decay" was found in Trotsky's desk after his assassination in August 1940. Its first English translation, by John G. Wright, appeared in *Fourth International,* February 1941. Slight revisions have been made in the translations of most of these selections.

The Question of Trade Union Unity

The question of the unity of the workers' organizations is not subject to a single solution suitable for all forms of organization and for all conditions.

The question resolves itself most categorically for the party. Its complete independence is the elementary condition of revolutionary action. But even this principle does not give in advance a ready-made reply to the questions: When and under what conditions must a split or, contrariwise, a unification be made with a neighboring political current? Such questions are settled each time on the basis of a concrete analysis of the tendencies and political conditions. The highest criterion, in any case, remains the necessity for the vanguard of the organized proletariat, the party, to preserve its complete independence and autonomy on the basis of a distinct program of action.

But precisely such a solution of the question with regard to the party not only admits but, as a general rule, renders indispensable a quite different attitude with regard to the question of the unity of other mass organizations of the working class: trade unions, cooperatives, soviets.

Each one of these organizations has its own tasks and methods of work — and, within certain limits, independent ones. For the Communist Party, all these organizations are first of all the arena of revolutionary education of broad sections of the workers and recruitment of the advanced workers. The larger the mass in a given organization, the greater are the possibilities it offers the revolutionary vanguard. That is why, as a rule, it is not the Communist wing but the reformist wing that takes the initiative in splitting the mass organizations.

It is enough to contrast the conduct of the Bolsheviks in 1917 to that of the British trade unions in recent years. The Bolsheviks not only remained in the same trade unions with the Mensheviks, but in certain trade unions they tolerated a Menshevik leadership even after the October Revolution, although the Bolsheviks had the overwhelming majority in the soviets. The British trade unions, on the contrary, upon the initiative of the Labourites, not only drive the Communists out of the Labour Party but, so far as it is possible, out of the trade unions as well.

In France, the split in the trade unions was also the consequence of the initiative of the reformists, and it is no accident that the revolutionary trade union organization, compelled to lead an independent existence, adopted the name *unitary*.[47]

Do we demand today that the Communists quit the ranks of the CGT? Not at all. On the contrary, the revolutionary wing within Jouhaux's confederation [CGT] must be strengthened. But by that alone we show that the splitting of the trade union organization is in no case a question of principle for us. All these ultraleftist objections in principle that may be formulated against trade union unity apply first of all to the participation of Communists in the CGT. Yet every revolutionist who has not lost touch with reality must recognize that the creation of Communist fractions in the reformist trade unions is an extremely important task. One of the tasks of these fractions must be the defense of the CGTU to the members of the reformist trade unions. This cannot be accomplished except by showing that the Communists do not want the trade unions to be split but, on the contrary, are ready at any moment to reestablish trade union unity.

If one believes for an instant that the splitting of the trade unions is imposed on Communists by their duty to counterpose a revolutionary policy to the policy of the reformists, then one cannot limit himself to France alone: One must demand that the Communists, regardless of the relationship of forces, break with the reformist trade unions and also set up their own trade unions in Germany, in England, in the United States, etc. In certain countries, the Communist parties have actually taken this road. In specific cases, the reformists really leave no other way out. In other cases, the Communists commit an obvious mistake by responding to the provocations of the reformists. But up to now, Communists have never and nowhere motivated the splitting of the trade unions by the inadmissibility in principle of working with the reformists in the organizations of the proletarian masses.

Without stopping to deal with cooperatives, the experiences in which will add nothing essential to what has been said above, we will take soviets as an example. These arise in one of the most revolutionary periods, when all problems are posed with the keenness of a blade. Can one, however, imagine even for a moment the creation of Communist soviets as a counterbalance to social-democratic soviets? This would mean killing the very idea of the soviets. At the beginning of 1917, the Bolsheviks remained within the soviets as an insignificant minority. For months — and in a period when months counted for years, if not for decades — the Bolsheviks tolerated a conciliationist majority in the soviets, even though they already represented an overwhelming majority in the factory committees. Finally, even after the conquest of power, the Bolsheviks tolerated the Mensheviks within the soviets while these latter represented a certain part of the working class. It was only when the Mensheviks had completely compromised and isolated themselves, by being transformed into a clique, that the soviets threw them out of their midst.

In Spain, where in the near future the slogan of soviets could already be put practically on the order of the day, the very creation of soviets (juntas), provided there is an energetic and bold initiative of the Communists, is not to be conceived of otherwise than by way of a technical organizational agreement with the trade unions and the socialists on the method and the intervals of the election of workers' representatives. To advance, under these conditions, the idea of the inadmissibility of working with the reformists in the mass organizations would be one of the most disastrous forms of sectarianism.

How then is such an attitude on our part towards the proletarian organizations led by the reformists to be reconciled with our evaluation of reformism as the left wing of the imperialist bourgeoisie? This contradiction is not a formal but a dialectical one, that is to say, one that flows from the very course of the class struggle. A considerable part of the working class (its majority in a number of countries) rejects our evaluation of reformism; in other countries, it has not as yet even approached this question. The whole problem consists precisely of leading these masses to revolutionary conclusions on the basis of our common experiences with them. We say to the non-Communist and to the anti-Communist workers: "Today you still believe in the reformist leaders whom we consider to be traitors. We cannot and we do not wish to impose our point of view upon you by force. We want to convince you. Let us then endeavor to fight together and to examine the methods and the results of these fights." This means: full freedom of groupings within the united trade unions where trade union discipline exists for all.

No other principled position can be proposed.

*　　*　　*

The Executive Committee of the Communist League [Left Opposition in France] is at present correctly giving first place to the question of the united front. This is the only way that one can prevent the reformists, and above all their left-wing agents, the Monattists, from counterposing to the practical tasks of the class struggle the formal slogan of unity. Vassart, [48] as a counterbalance to the sterile official line, has put forward the idea of the united front with the local trade union organizations. This way of posing the question is correct, in the sense that during local strikes it is primarily a question of working with local trade unions and specific federations. It is equally true that the lower links of the reformist apparatus are more sensitive to the pressure of the workers. But it would be wrong to make any kind of principled difference between agreements with the local opportunists and those with their chiefs. Everything depends upon the conditions of the moment, upon the strength of the pressure of the masses, and upon the character of the tasks which are on the order of the day.

It is self-understood that we in no case put the agreement with the reformists, whether locally or centrally, as the indispensable and pre-

48

liminary condition for the struggle in each specific case. We do not orient ourselves according to the reformists but according to the objective circumstances and the state of mind of the masses. The same applies to the character of demands put forward. It would be fatal for us to engage ourselves in advance to accept the united front according to the conditions of the reformists, that is, upon the basis of minimal demands. The working masses will not rise for the struggle in the name of demands that would seem fantastic to them. But on the other hand, should the demands be too limited in advance, then the workers may say to themselves: "The game is not worth the candle."

The task does not consist of each time proposing the united front formally to the reformists, but of imposing conditions upon them which correspond as best as possible to the situation. All this calls for an active and maneuverist strategy. In any case, it is incontestable that it is particularly and only in this way that the CGTU can mitigate, up to a certain point, the consequences of dividing the masses into two trade union organizations, that it can throw the responsibility for the split upon those on whom it really belongs, and put forward its own positions of struggle.

The singularity of the situation in France lies in the fact that two trade union organizations have existed there separately for many years. In the face of the ebb of the movement in recent years, people have accustomed themselves to the split; very often it has simply been forgotten. However, one could foresee that the revival in the ranks of the working class would inevitably revive the slogan of the unity of the trade union organizations. If one takes into account that more than nine-tenths of the French proletariat is outside the trade unions, it becomes clear that, with this revival being accentuated, the pressure of the unorganized will increase. The slogan of unity is nothing but one of the first consequences of this pressure. With a correct policy, this pressure should be favorable to the Communist Party and the CGTU.

If, for the next period, an active united-front policy were the principle method of the French Communists' trade union strategy, it would be a complete mistake nonetheless to counterpose the policy of united front to the policy of unity of the trade union organizations.

It is entirely incontestable that the unity of the working class can be realized only on a revolutionary basis. The policy of the united front is one of the means of liberating the workers from reformist influence and even, in the last analysis, of moving towards the genuine unity of the working class. We must constantly explain this Marxian truth to the advanced workers. But a historical perspective, even the most correct one, cannot replace the living experience of the masses. The party is the vanguard, but in its work, especially in its trade union work, it must be able to lean towards the rearguard. It must, in fact, show the workers — once, twice, and even ten times if necessary — that it is ready at any moment at all to help them reconstitute the unity of the trade union organizations. And in this field, we remain faithful to the essential principles of Marxian strategy: the combining of the struggle for reforms with the struggle for revolution.

What is the attitude today of the two trade union confederations towards unity? To the broad circles of the workers, it must appear entirely identical. In truth, the administrative stratum of each organization has declared that unification can only be conceived of "from below" on the basis of that organization's principles. By covering itself with the slogan of unity from below, borrowed from the CGTU, the reformist confederation exploits the forgetfulness of the working class and the ignorance of the younger generation which knows nothing of the splitting work of Jouhaux, Dumoulin and Company. At the same time, the Monattists assist Jouhaux by substituting for the fighting tasks of the labor movement the single slogan of trade union unity. As honest courtiers, they direct all their efforts against the CGTU in order to detach from it the greatest possible number of trade unions, to group them around themselves, and then to enter into negotiations with the reformist confederation on an equal footing.

As far as I am able to judge here from the material I have, Vassart has expressed himself in favor of the Communists themselves putting forward the slogan of a unification congress of the two trade union confederations. This proposal was categorically rejected; as for its author, he was accused of having gone over to Monatte's position. Lacking data, I am unable to express myself thoroughly on this discussion. But I consider that the French Communists have no reason to abandon the slogan of a fusion congress. On the contrary.

The Monattists say: "They are both, one as much as the other, splitters. We alone are for unity. Workers, support us." The reformists reply: "As for us, we are for unity from below." That is, "we" will generously permit the workers to rejoin our organization. What must the revolutionary confederation say on this subject? "It is not for nothing that we call ourselves the *unitary* confederation. We are ready to effect the unity of the trade union organization this very day. But to accomplish that, the workers have no need whatsoever of suspicious courtiers who have no trade union organization behind them and who feed upon splits like maggots on a festering wound. We propose the preparation and, after a specified period, the convening of a fusion congress on the basis of trade union democracy."

This manner of posing the question would have immediately cut the ground from under the feet of the Monattists, who are a completely sterile political grouping but capable of bringing great confusion into the ranks of the proletariat. But will not this liquidation of the group of courtiers cost us too dearly? It will be objected that, in case the reformists should consent to a unity congress, the Communists would be in the minority there and the CGTU would have to yield its place to the CGT.

Such a consideration can appear persuasive only to a left trade union bureaucrat who is fighting for his " independence" while losing sight of the perspectives and tasks of the movement as a whole. The unity of the two trade union organizations, even if the revolutionary wing remains in the minority for a time, would show itself in a short period of time to be favorable precisely to communism and only to communism. The unity of the confederations would bring in its train a great influx of new members. Thanks to this, the influence of the crisis would be reflected within the trade unions in a more profound and more decisive fashion. The left wing would be able, within the rising new wave, to begin a decisive struggle for the conquest of the unified confederation. A sure majority in a narrow and isolated trade union confederation, rather than oppositional work in a broad and real mass organization, can be preferred only by sectarians or officials but not by proletarian revolutionists.

For a thinking Marxist, it is quite evident that one of the reasons contributing to the monstrous mistakes of the CGTU leadership resulted from a situation where people like Monmousseau, Semard, and others, without theoretical preparation or revolutionary experience, immediately proclaimed themselves the "masters" of an independent organization and consequently had the possibility of experimenting with it under the orders of Losovsky, Manuilsky and Company. [49] It is incontestable that if the reformists had not at some point brought about the split in the confederation, Monmousseau and Company would have had to reckon with broader masses. This fact alone would have disciplined their bureaucratic adventurism. That is why the advantages of unity would have been immeasurably greater at present than the disadvantages. If, within a unified confederation embracing about a million workers, the revolutionary wing remains in the minority for a year or two, these two years would undoubtedly be more fruitful for the education not only of the Communist trade unionists, but for the whole party, than five years of "independent" zigzags in a CGTU growing constantly weaker.

No, it is not we but the reformists who should fear trade union unity. If they consent to a unity congress — not in words but in fact — that would create the possibility of bringing the labor movement in France out of its blind alley. But that is just why the reformists will not consent to it.

The conditions of the crisis are creating the greatest difficulties for the reformists, primarily in the trade union field. That is why they find it so necessary to take shelter behind their left flank; it is the courtiers of unity who offer them this shelter.

To unmask the splitting work of the reformists and the parasitism of the Monattists is now one of the most important and indispensable tasks. The slogan of the unity congress can contribute greatly to the solution of this task. When the Monattists speak of unity, they aim this slogan against the Communists; when the CGTU itself proposes a road to unity, it will deliver a mortal blow to the Monattists and will weaken the reformists. Isn't this quite clear?

It is true that we know in advance that, thanks to the resistance of the reformists, the slogan of unity will not yield the great results at present that would be obtained in the case of a real unity of the trade union organizations. But a more limited result, provided the Communists follow a correct policy, will undoubtedly be achieved. The broad masses of workers will see who is really for unity and who is against it, and will become convinced that the services of courtiers are not required. There is no doubt that in the long run the Monattists will be reduced to nothing, the CGTU will feel itself stronger, and the CGT weaker and more unstable.

But if that is how matters stand, then does it not amount only to a maneuver rather than to the achieving of effective unity? This objection cannot frighten us. This is the manner in which the reformists especially evaluate our whole policy of the united front: they declare that our proposals are a maneuver only because they themselves do not want to lead the struggle.

It would be entirely false to make any difference in principle between the policy of the united front and that of the fusion of the trade union organizations. Provided that the Communists preserve the complete independence of their party, of their fraction in the trade unions, of their whole policy, the fusion of the confederations is nothing but a form of the policy of the united front, a more extended and broader form. In rejecting our proposal, the reformists transform it into a "maneuver." But on our part, it is a legitimate and indispensable "maneuver"; it is such maneuvers that train the working masses.

*   *   *

The Executive Committee of the Communist League, we say again, is entirely correct when it urgently repeats that unity of action cannot be postponed until the unification of the trade union organizations. This idea must be developed as it has been heretofore, explained, and applied in practice. But this does not exclude the duty of posing boldly, at a definite and well-chosen moment, the question of the fusion of the confederations (or even of single federations).

The whole question consists of knowing if the Communist leadership is now capable of effecting such a bold maneuver. The future will show. But if the [Communist] party and the leadership of the CGTU refuse to follow the advice of the League today—which is most probable—it may well be that they will be obliged to follow it tomorrow. It is superfluous to add that we make no fetish of trade union unity. We postpone no question of struggle until unity. It is not a question for us of a panacea, but of a lesson in specific and important things that must be taught to the workers who have forgotten or who do not know the past.

For participation in the unity congress, we do not of course set any conditions of principle.

When the courtiers of unity, who are not ashamed of cheap phrases, say that the united confederation must base itself upon the principle of class struggle, etc., they are doing verbal acrobatics in the interests of the opportunists. As if a serious man could ask Jouhaux and Company to tread, in the name of unity with the Communists, the road of the class struggle which these gentlemen have deliberately abandoned in the name of unity with the bourgeoisie. And just what do these courtiers themselves, all these Monattes, Zyromskys, and Dumoulins, understand by the "class struggle"? No, we are ready at any moment to stand on the grounds of trade union unity, not in order to "correct" (with the aid of quack formulas) the mercenaries of capital, but in order to tear the workers away from their traitorous influence. The only conditions that we set have the character of organizational guarantees of trade union democracy, first of all the freedom of criticism for the minority, naturally on the condition that it submits to trade union discipline. We ask for nothing else, and on our part we promise nothing more.

Let us imagine that the [Communist] party—even if not immediately—follows our advice. How should its Central Committee act? It would first of all be obliged carefully to prepare within the party the plan of campaign, to discuss it in all the trade union fractions in the light of local trade union conditions so that the slogan of unity might be effectively directed simultaneously from above and from below. Only after careful preparation and elaboration, after having eliminated all doubts and misunderstandings within its own ranks, would the leadership of the CGTU address itself to the leadership of the reformist confederation with concretely elaborated proposals: to create a parity commission for the preparation, within a period of two months for example, of the trade union unification congress to which all the trade union organizations of the country must have access. Simultaneously, the local CGTU organizations address themselves to the local CGT organizations with the same proposal, formulated with precision and concreteness.

The Communist Party would develop a broad agitation in the country, supporting and explaining the initiative of the CGTU. The attention of the broadest circles of workers, and primarily that of the CGT workers, must for a certain time be concentrated on the simple idea that the Communists propose to achieve immediately the organizational unity of the trade union organizations. Whatever the attitude of the reformists may be, whatever may be the ruses to which they resort, the Communists will come out of this campaign with profit, even if their proposal comes to no more, in this first attempt, than a demonstration of their attitude.

The struggle in the name of the united front does not cease, during this period, for a single minute. The Communists continue to attack the reformists in the provinces and in the center, basing themselves upon the growing activity of the workers, renewing all their offers of fighting actions on the basis of the policy of the united front, unmasking the reformists, strengthening their own ranks, etc. And it may well happen that in six months, in a year or two, the Communists will be obliged to repeat their proposal of fusion of the trade union confederations and thus put the reformists in a more difficult position than the first time.

The real Bolshevik policy must have precisely this character which at the same time takes the offensive, is bold and maneuverist. It is only on this road that the movement can be preserved from stagnation, purged of parasitic formations, and the evolution of the working class towards revolution can be accelerated.

The lesson proposed above has no meaning and cannot succeed unless the initiative comes from the CGTU and the Communist Party. The task of the League naturally does not consist of independently advancing the slogan of a unity congress, pitting itself against the CGTU as well as against the CGT. The League's task is to push the official [Communist] party and the CGTU onto the road of a bold united front policy and to stimulate them — on the basis of this policy — to carry out at a propitious moment, and in the future there will be many such moments, a decisive offensive for the fusion of the trade union organizations.

In order to fulfill its tasks towards the [Communist] party, the League — and this is its first duty — must align its own ranks in the field of the trade union movement. It is a task that cannot be postponed. It must and will be solved.

March 25, 1931

The Unions in Britain

. . . The trade union question remains the most important question of proletarian policy in Great Britain, as well as in the majority of old capitalist countries. The mistakes of the Comintern in this field are innumerable. No wonder: a party's inability to establish correct relations with the class reveals itself most glaringly in the area of the trade union movement. That is why I consider it necessary to dwell on this question.

The trade unions were formed during the period of the growth and rise of capitalism. They had as their task the raising of the material and cultural level of the proletariat and the extension of its political rights. This work, which in England lasted over a century, gave the trade unions tremendous authority among the workers. The decay of British capitalism, under the conditions of decline of the world capitalist system, undermined the basis for the reformist work of the trade unions. Capitalism can continue to maintain itself only by lowering the standard of living of the working class. Under these conditions trade unions can either transform themselves into revolutionary organizations or become lieutenants of capital in the intensified exploitation of the workers. The trade union bureaucracy, which has satisfactorily solved its own social problem, took the second path. It turned all the accumulated authority of the trade unions against the socialist revolution and even against any attempts of the workers to resist the attacks of capital and reaction.

From that point on, the most important task of the revolutionary party became the liberation of the workers from the reactionary influence of the trade union bureaucracy. In this decisive field the Comintern revealed complete inadequacy. In 1926-27, especially in the period of the miners' strike and the General Strike, that is, at the time of the greatest crimes and betrayals of the General Council of the trade unions, the Comintern obsequiously toadied to the highly placed strikebreakers, cloaked them with its authority in the eyes of the masses, and helped them remain in the saddle. That is how the Minority Movement was struck a mortal blow. Frightened by the results of its own work, the Comintern bureaucracy went to the extreme of ultraradicalism. The fatal excesses of the "third period"[50] were due to the desire of the small Communist minority to act as though it had a majority behind it. Isolating itself more and more from the working class, the Communist Party counterposed to the trade unions, which embraced millions of workers, its own trade union organizations, highly obedient to the leadership of the Comintern but separated by an abyss from the working class. No better favor could be done for the trade union bureaucracy. Had it been with its power to award the Order of the Garter, it should have so decorated all the leaders of the Comintern and Profintern.[51]

As was said, the trade unions now play not a progressive but a reactionary role. Nevertheless they still embrace millions of workers. One must not think that the workers are blind and do not see the change in the historic role of the trade unions. But what is to be done? The revolutionary road is seriously compromised in the eyes of the left wing of the workers by the zigzags and adventures of official communism. The workers say to themselves: The trade unions are bad, but without them it might be even worse. This is the psychology of being in a blind alley. Meanwhile, the trade union bureaucracy persecutes the revolutionary workers ever more boldly, ever more impudently replacing internal democracy by the arbitrary action of a clique, in essence transforming the trade unions into some sort of concentration camp for the workers during the decline of capitalism.

Under these conditions, the thought easily arises: Is it not possible to bypass the trade unions? Is it not possible to replace them by some sort of fresh, uncorrupted organization of the type of revolutionary trade unions, shop committes, soviets, and the like? The fundamental mistake of such attempts lies in that they reduce to organizational experiments the great political problem of how to free the masses from the influence of the trade union bureaucracy. It is not enough to offer the masses a new address. It is necessary to seek out the masses where they are and to lead them.

Impatient leftists sometimes say that it is absolutely impossible to win over the trade unions because the bureaucracy uses the organizations' internal regimes for preserving its own interests, resorting to the basest machinations, repressions and plain crookedness, in the spirit of the parliamentary oligarchy of the era of "rotten boroughs." Why then waste time and energy? This argument reduces itself in reality to giving up the actual struggle to win the masses, using the corrupt character of the trade union bureaucracy as a pretext. This argument can be developed further: Why not abandon revolutionary work altogether, considering the repressions and provocations on the part of the government bureaucracy? There exists no principled difference here, since the trade union bureaucracy has definitely become a part of the capitalist apparatus, economic and governmental. It is absurd to think that it would be possible to work against the trade union bureaucracy with its own help, or only with its consent. Insofar as it defends itself by persecutions, violence, expulsions, frequently resorting to the assistance of government authorities, we must learn to work in the trade unions *discreetly*, finding a common language with the masses but not revealing ourselves prematurely to the bureaucracy. It is precisely in the present epoch, when the reformist bureaucracy of the proletariat has transformed itself into the economic police of capital, that revolutionary work in the trade unions, performed intelligently and systematically, may yield decisive results in a comparatively short time.

We do not at all mean by this that the revolutionary party has any guarantee that the trade unions will be completely won over to the socialist revolution. The problem is not so simple. The trade union apparatus has attained for itself great independence from the masses. The bureaucracy is capable of retaining its positions a long time after the masses have turned against it. But it is precisely such a situation, where the masses are already hostile to the trade union bureaucracy but where the bureaucracy is still capable of misrepresenting the opinion of the organization and of sabotaging new elections, that is most favorable for the creation of shop committees, workers' councils, and other organizations for the immediate needs of any given moment. Even in Russia, where the trade unions did not have anything like the powerful traditions of the British trade unions, the October Revolution occurred with Mensheviks predominant in the administration of the trade unions. Having lost the masses, these administrations were still capable of sabotaging elections in the apparatus, although already powerless to sabotage the proletarian revolution.

It is absolutely necessary right now to prepare the minds of the advanced workers for the idea of creating shop committees and workers' councils at the moment of a sharp change. But it would be the greatest mistake to "play around" in practice with the slogan of shop councils, consoling oneself, with this "idea," for the lack of real work and real influence in the trade unions. To counterpose to the existing trade unions the abstract idea of workers' councils would mean setting against oneself not only the bureaucracy but also the masses, thus depriving oneself of the possibility of preparing the ground for the creation of workers' councils.

In this the Comintern has gained not a little experience: having created obedient, that is, purely Communist trade unions, it counterposed its sections to the working masses in a hostile manner and thereby doomed itself to complete impotence. This is one of the most important causes of the collapse of the German Communist Party. It is true that the British Communist Party, insofar as I am informed, opposes the slogan of workers' councils under the present conditions. Superficially, this may seem like a realistic appraisal of the situation. In reality, the British Communist Party rejects only *one form* of political adventurism for *another*, more hysterical form. The theory and practice of social-fascism[52] and the rejection of the policy of the united front creates insurmountable obstacles to working in the trade unions, since each trade union is, by its very nature, the arena of an ongoing united front of revolutionary parties with reformist and non-party masses. To the extent that the British Communist Party proved incapable, even after the German tragedy, of learning anything and arming itself anew, to that extent can an alliance with it pull to the bottom even the ILP, which only recently has entered a period of revolutionary apprenticeship.

Pseudo-Communists will, no doubt, refer to the last congress of trade unions, which declared that there could be no united front with Communists against fascism. It would be the greatest folly to accept this piece of wisdom as the final verdict of history. The trade union bureaucrats can permit themselves such boastful formulas only because they are not immediately threatened by fascism, or by Communism. When the hammer of fascism is raised over the head of the trade unions, then, with a correct policy of the revolutionary party, the trade union masses will show an irresistible urge for an alliance with the revolutionary wing and will carry with them onto this path even a certain portion of the apparatus. Contrariwise, if Communism should become a decisive force, threatening the General Councils with the loss of positions, honors, and income, Messrs. Citrine[53] and Company would undoubtedly enter into a bloc with Mosley[54] and Company against the Communists. Thus, in August 1917, the Russian Mensheviks and Social-Revolutionaries together with the Bolsheviks repulsed General Kornilov. Two months later, in October, they were fighting hand in hand with the Kornilovists against the Bolsheviks. And in the first months of 1917, when the reformists were still strong, they spouted, just like Citrine and Company, about the impossibility of them making an alliance with a dictatorship either of the right or left.

The revolutionary proletarian party must be welded together by a clear understanding of its historic tasks. This presupposes a scientifically based program. At the same time, the revolutionary party must know how to establish correct relations with the class. This presupposes a policy of revolutionary realism, equally removed from opportunistic vagueness and sectarian aloofness. From the point of view of both these closely connected criteria, the ILP should review its relation to the Comintern as well as to all other organizations and tendencies within the working class. This concerns first of all the fate of the ILP itself.

September 4, 1933

Letters on the Dutch Union Situation

July 16, 1936

To the Central Committee of the RSAP[55]
Amsterdam

. . . b) On the trade union question too I cannot share the policy of our Dutch brother party. The reasons therefor I have often set forth in writing and especially verbally. The NAS[56] policy continues to be carried out only on the basis of the law of inertia. There is no deeper strategic motivation for it. The development in Holland, just as is now the case in France, will have to strike out either on the revolutionary or the fascist road. In either case I see no place for the NAS. When the great strike wave will begin in Holland, which should be regarded as highly probable if not certain, the reformist trade unions will grow mightily, absorb fresh elements into their ranks, and in such a period the NAS will appear to the masses as an incomprehensible splinter organization. In consequence, the masses will also become unresponsive to the correct slogans of the RSAP and the leadership of the NAS. But if all the members of the RSAP and the best NAS elements were inside the reformist trade unions, then during the impending upsurge they could become the axis of crystallization of the left wing

58

and, later on, the decisive force in the labor movement. I must say quite openly: the systematic, solicitously arranged agitation inside the reformist trade unions seems to me the only means not only of preserving the RSAP as a genuinely independent party (for by itself this hasn't any historical value), but also of carrying it to victory, that is, to power.

If we take a much less probable alternative, namely, that the development in Holland, without passing through a revolutionary upsurge, goes directly, in the coming period, into the reactionary military-bureaucratic and then into the fascist phase, we nevertheless come to the same conclusion: The NAS policy must become an obstacle to the party. The first assault of the reaction has already been directed at the NAS and cost it half its membership. The second assault will cost it its life. The excellent workers united within it will then have to seek the road into the reformist trade unions in a dispersed manner, everyone for himself, or else remain passive and indifferent. The trade union cannot lead the illegal existence that the party can. But by means of this blow the party will be terribly hit, for an illegal revolutionary party must have a legal and semilegal mass cover. If the bulk of the membership of the RSAP is active in the reformist trade unions, then these mass organizations signify also for the party a hiding place, a cover and, at the same time, an arena. The coherence of the present NAS workers is thereby preserved. All other points will be conditioned by the course of development and the policy of the party.

*　　*　　*

December 2, 1937

To Sneevliet[57]

. . . You must finally understand that nobody in our international movement is inclined to further tolerate the absolutely abnormal situation under which the Dutch party covers itself with the banner of the Fourth International and conducts a policy which is flagrantly contradictory to all our principles and decisions.

The NAS has definitely become a stone around the neck of the party, and this stone will drag you to the bottom. A party that doesn't participate in the real trade unions is not a revolutionary party. The NAS exists only thanks to the toleration and financial support of the bourgeois government. This financial support is dependent upon your political attitude. That is the genuine reason why the party didn't, in spite of all our insistence, elaborate a political platform. That is also the reason why you, as parliamentary deputy, never gave a genuine revolutionary speech which could serve for propaganda in Holland as well as abroad. Your activity has a diplomatic and not a very revolutionary character. You are bound through your NAS position by the hands and by the feet. And the NAS itself is not a bridge to the masses but a wall separating you from the masses.

When we criticized false trade union politics in other countries, people answer: "And your Dutch organization?" . . . Do you believe that any serious revolutionary organization can tolerate indefinitely such a situation? We are very patient, but we cannot sacrifice the elementary interests of our movement.

*   *   *

January 21, 1938

To the International Secretariat,
Copy to all Sections

. . . All that the IS has written about and against Sneevliet was and still is absolutely correct. That is precisely the reason why Sneevliet has never dared to respond with political arguments, utilizing instead, and that is his manner, abusive language absolutely intolerable and not at all justified. Sneevliet does not take the least interest in Marxism, in theories, in a general orientation. What interests him is the NAS, a tiny bureaucratic machine, a parliamentary post. Sneevliet utilizes the banner of the Fourth International above all in order to protect his opportunistic work in Holland. Since the NAS depends financially entirely upon the government, Sneevliet has evaded all precise politics, that is to say, Marxist politics, in order not to provoke the thunder of the government against the NAS. The RSAP has been and still is nothing more than a political appendage of the NAS, which itself is not viable and which has fallen in the last years from 25,000 to 12,000 members and very likely still lower.

Trade Unions in the Transitional Epoch

In the struggle for partial and transitional demands, the workers now more than ever before need mass organizations, principally trade unions. The powerful growth of trade unionism in France and the United States is the best refutation of the preachments of those ultraleft doctrinaires who have been teaching that trade unions have "outlived their usefulness."

The Bolshevik-Leninist stands in the frontline trenches of all kinds of struggles, even when they involve only the most modest material interests or democratic rights of the working class. He takes active part in mass trade unions for the purpose of strengthening them and raising their spirit of militancy. He fights uncompromisingly against any attemp to subordinate the unions to the bourgeois state and bind the proletariat to "compulsory arbitration" and every other form of police guardianship—not only fascist but also "democratic." Only on the basis of such work within the trade unions is successful struggle possible against the reformists, including those of the Stalinist bureaucracy. Sectarian attempts to build or preserve small "revolutionary" unions, as a second edition of the party, signify in actuality the renouncing of the struggle for leadership of the working class. It is necessary to establish this firm rule: self-isolation of the capitulationist variety from mass trade unions, which is tantamount to a betrayal of the revolution, is incompatible with membership in the Fourth International.

*　　*　　*

At the same time, the Fourth International resolutely rejects and condemns trade union fetishism, equally characteristic of trade unionists and syndicalists.

(a) Trade unions do not offer and, in line with their task, composition, and manner of recruiting membership, cannot offer a finished revolutionary program; in consequence, they cannot replace the *party*. The building of national revolutionary parties as sections of the Fourth International is the central task of the transitional epoch.

(b) Trade unions, even the most powerful, embrace no more than 20 to 25 per cent of the working class, and at that, predominantly the more skilled and better-paid layers. The more oppressed majority of the working class is drawn only episodically into the struggle, during a period of exceptional upsurges in the labor movement. During such moments it is necessary to create organizations *ad hoc*, embracing the whole fighting mass: strike committees, factory committees, and finally, soviets.

(c) As organizations expressive of the top layers of the proletariat, trade unions, as witnessed by all past historical experience, including the fresh experience of the anarcho-syndicalist unions in Spain, developed powerful tendencies toward compromise with the bourgeois-democratic regime. In periods of acute class struggle, the leading bodies of the trade unions aim to become masters of the mass movement in order to render it harmless. This is already occurring during the period of simple strikes, especially in the case of the mass sit-down strikes which shake the principle of bourgeois property. In time of war or revolution, when the bourgeoisie is plunged into exceptional difficulties, the trade union leaders usually become bourgeois ministers.

Therefore, the sections of the Fourth International should always strive not only to renew the top leadership of the trade unions, boldly and resolutely in critical moments advancing new militant leaders in place of routine functionaries and careerists, but also to create in all possible instances independent militant organizations corresponding more closely to the tasks of mass struggle against bourgeois society; and if necessary, not flinching even in the face of a direct break with the conservative apparatus of the trade unions. If it be criminal to turn one's back on mass organizations for the sake of fostering sectarian fictions, it is no less so to passively tolerate subordination of the revolutionary mass movement to the control of openly reactionary or disguised conservative ("progressive") bureaucratic cliques. Trade unions are not ends in themselves; they are but means along the road to proletarian revolution.

Factory Committees

During a transitional epoch, the workers' movement does not have a systematic and well balanced, but a feverish and explosive character. Slogans as well as organizational forms should be subordinated to the indices of the movement. On guard against routine handling of a situation as against a plague, the leadership should respond sensitively to the initiative of the masses.

Sit-down strikes, the latest expression of this kind of initiative, go beyond the limits of "normal" capitalist procedure. Independently of the demands of the strikers, the temporary seizure of factories deals a blow to the idol, capitalist property. Every sit-down strike poses in a practical manner the question of who is boss of the factory: the capitalist or the workers?

If the sit-down strike raises this question episodically, the *factory committee* gives it organized expression. Elected by all the factory employees, the factory committee immediately creates a counterweight to the will of the administration.

To the reformist criticism of bosses of the so-called "economic royalist" type like Ford in contradistinction to "good," "democratic" exploiters, we counterpose the slogan of factory committees as centers of struggle against both the first and the second.

Trade union bureaucrats will as a general rule resist the creation of factory committees, just as they resist every bold step taken along the road of mobilizing the masses.

However, the wider the sweep of the movement, the easier will it be to break this resistance. Where the closed shop has already been instituted in "peaceful" times, the committee will formally coincide with the usual organ of the trade union, but will renew its personnel and widen its functions. The prime significance of the committee, however, lies in the fact that it becomes the militant staff for such working-class layers as the trade union is usually incapable of moving to action. It is precisely from these more oppressed layers that the most self-sacrificing battalions of the revolution will come.

From the moment that the committee makes its appearance, a factual dual power is established in the factory. By its very essence it represents the transitional state, because it includes in itself two irreconcilable regimes: the capitalist and the proletarian. The fundamental significance of factory committees is precisely contained in the fact that they open the doors if not to a direct revolutionary, then to a prerevolutionary period — between the bourgeois and the proletarian regimes. That the propagation of the factory committee idea is neither premature nor artificial is amply attested to by the waves of sit-down strikes spreading through several countries. New waves of this type will be inevitable in the immediate future. It is necessary to begin a campaign in favor of factory committees in time, in order not to be caught unawares.

April 1938

Discussion With a CIO Organizer

[In September 1938, Trotsky was visited at his home in Mexico by a CIO official from the United States. Their discussion was taken down by a stenographer. Preceded by a brief editorial note signed "Crux," a pen name of Trotsky, "that part of the discussion which may be of general interest" appeared in the Russian-language *Bulletin of the Opposition* of November, 1938. Names were not used in the transcript, the American trade union official being identified merely as "A" and "one of the foreign activists of the Fourth International" — actually Trotsky — being identified as "B."]

* * *

A: Our union's policies are aimed at preventing complete unemployment. We have got the work spread out among all the members of the union with no reduction in the hourly rate of pay.

B: And what percentage of their former total wages do your workers now get?

A: About 40 per cent.

B: Why that's monstrous! You've won a sliding scale of working hours, with no change in the hourly rate of pay? But that only means that the full burden of unemployment falls with all its weight on the workers themselves. You free the bourgeoisie from the need of spending its resources on the unemployed by having each worker sacrifice three-fifths of his total wages.

A: There's a grain of truth in that. But what can be done?

B: Not a grain, but the whole truth! American capitalism is sick with a chronic and incurable disease. Can you console your workers with the hope that the present crisis will have a transitory character and that a new era of prosperity will open in the near future?

A: Personally, I don't allow myself such illusions. Many in our circles understand that capitalism has entered its era of decline.

B: But of course this means that tomorrow your workers will get 30 per cent of their former wages; the day after, 25 per cent, and so forth. Episodic improvements, it is true, are possible, even inevitable; but the overall curve is toward decline, degradation, impoverishment. Marx and Engels predicted this even in the *Communist Manifesto*. What is the program of your union and the CIO as a whole?

A: Unfortunately, you don't know the psychology of the American workers. They are not used to thinking about the future. They are interested in only one thing: what can be done now, immediately. Among the leaders of the trade union movement there are, of course, those who clearly take into account the dangers that threaten. But they can't change the psychology of the masses all at once. The habits, traditions, and views of the American workers tie them down and limit what they can do. All this can't be changed in a day.

B: Are you sure that history will provide you with years enough in which to prepare? The crisis of American capitalism has "American" tempos and proportions. A sturdy organism that has not known sickness before begins to deteriorate very rapidly at a certain point. The disintegration of capitalism means, at the same time, a direct and immediate threat to democracy, without which the trade unions cannot exist. Do you think, for example, that Mayor Hague* is just an accident?

A: Oh, no, I don't think so at all. I have had quite a few meetings in the recent period with trade union officials on this subject. My opinion is that in every state we already have — under one banner or another — a ready-made reactionary organization that can become a support for fascism on the national level. We don't have to wait fifteen or twenty years. Fascism can conquer among us in three or four.

B: In that case what is . . . . ?

A: Our program? I understand your question. It is a difficult situation; some major steps are necessary. But I don't see the necessary forces or necessary leaders for this.

B: Then does that mean capitulation without a fight?

A: It's a difficult situation. I have to admit that the majority of union activists don't see, or don't want to see, the danger. Our unions, as you know, have had an extraordinary growth in a short time. It's natural for the CIO chiefs to have a honeymoon psychology. They are inclined to view difficulties lightly. The government not only has

---

*The Mayor of Jersey City, who successfully applied purely fascistic methods against workers' organizations. [L.T.]

them figured out, but even plays with them. They are not used to this from past experience. It's natural that their heads spin a little. This pleasant dizziness is not conducive to critical thinking. They are tasting the joys of today without worrying about tomorrow.

B: Well said! On this I agree with you completely. But the success of the CIO is temporary. It is merely a symptom of the fact that the working class of the United States has begun to move, has broken out of its routine, is hunting for new ways to save itself from the threatening abyss. If your unions do not find new ways, they will be ground to dust. Hague is already stronger than Lewis; because Hague, despite his limited situation, knows exactly what he wants, while Lewis doesn't. Things may end up with your chiefs waking from their "pleasant dizziness" to find themselves — in concentration camps.

A: Unfortunately, the past history of the United States with its unlimited opportunities, its individualism, has not taught our workers to think socially. It's enough to tell you that at best 15 per cent of the organized workers come to union meetings. That's something to think about.

B: But perhaps the reason for the absenteeism of 85 per cent is that the speakers have nothing to say to the ranks?

A: Hmm. That's true to a certain extent. The economic situation is such that we are forced to hold back the workers, to put brakes on the movement, to retreat. This is not to the workers' liking, of course.

B: Here we have the heart of the matter. It is not the ranks who are to blame but the leaders. In the classical epoch of capitalism the trade unions also got into difficult situations during crises and were forced to retreat, lost part of their membership, spent their reserve funds. But then there was at least the assurance that the next upturn would allow the losses to be made up, and more besides. Today there isn't the slightest hope for such a thing. The unions will go down step by step. Your organization, the CIO, may collapse as quickly as it arose.

A: What can be done?

B: Above all, one must tell the masses what's what. It's inadmissible to play hide-and-seek. You, of course, know the American workers better than I. Nevertheless, let me assure you that you are looking at them through old eyeglasses. The masses are immeasurably better, more daring and resolute than the leaders. The very fact of the rapid rise of the CIO shows that the American worker has changed radically under the impact of the terrible economic jolts of the postwar period, especially of the past decade. When you showed a little initiative in building more combative unions, the workers immediately responded and gave you extraordinary, unprecedented support. You have no right to complain about the masses. And what about the so-called sit-down strikes? It wasn't the leaders who thought them up, but the workers themselves. Isn't this an unmistakable sign that the American workers are ready to go over to more decisive methods of combat? Mayor Hague is a direct product of the sit-down strikes. Unfortunately, no one in the top layer of the trade unions has yet dared to deduce from the sharpening of the social struggle such daring conclusions as capitalist reaction has. This is the key to the situation. The leaders of capital think and act immeasurably more firmly, consistently, daringly, than do the leaders of the proletariat— these skeptics, routinists, bureaucrats, who are smothering the fighting spirit of the masses. It is from this that grows the danger of a victory for fascism, even in a very short time. The workers don't come to your meetings because they instinctively feel the insufficiency, the lack of substance, the lifelessness, the outright falsity of your program. The trade union leaders give out with platitudes at the very moment when every worker senses catastrophe overhead. One must find the language that corresponds to the real conditions of decaying capitalism and not to bureaucratic illusions.

A: I have already said that I see no leaders. There are separate groups, sects, but I see no one who could unite the worker masses, even if I agree with you that the masses are ready for struggle.

B: The problem is not leaders, but program. The correct program not only arouses and consolidates the masses, but also trains the leaders.

A: What do you consider a correct program?

B: You know that I am a Marxist; more precisely, a Bolshevik. My program has a very short and simple name: *socialist revolution.* But I don't ask that the leaders of the union movement immediately adopt the program of the Fourth International. What I do ask is that they draw conclusions from their work, from their own situation; that for themselves and for the masses they answer just these two questions: 1) How to save the CIO from bankruptcy and destruction? 2) How to save the United States from fascism?

A: What would you yourself do in the United States today if you were a trade union organizer?

B: First of all, the trade unions should stand the question of unemployment and wages on its head. The sliding scale of hours, such as you have, is correct: everyone should have work. But the sliding scale of hours should be supplemented by a sliding scale of wages. The working class cannot permit a continuous lowering of its living standards, for this would be equivalent to the destruction of human culture. The highest weekly pay rates on the eve of the 1929 crisis must be taken as the point of departure. The mighty productive forces created by the workers have not disappeared nor been destroyed; they are there at hand. Those who own and control these productive forces are responsible for unemployment. The workers know how to work and want to work. The work should be divided up among all the workers. The weekly pay for each worker should be no less than the maximum attained in the past. Such is the natural, the necessary, the unpostponable demand of the trade unions. Otherwise they will be swept away like trash by historical developments.

A: Is this program realizable? It means the certain ruin of the capitalists. This very program might hasten the growth of fascism.

B: Of course this program means struggle and not prostration. The trade unions have two possibilities: either to maneuver, tack back and forth, retreat, close their eyes and capitulate bit by bit in order not to "anger" the owners or "provoke" reaction. It was by this road that the German and Austrian social democrats and trade union officials tried to save themselves from fascism. The result is known to you: they cut their own throats. The other road is to understand the inexorable character of the present social crisis and to lead the masses to the offensive.

A: But you still haven't answered the question about fascism, that is, the immediate danger that the trade unions draw down upon themselves by radical demands.

B: I have not forgotten that for a moment. The fascist danger is already at hand, even before the appearance of radical demands. It flows from the decline and disintegration of capitalism. Granted that it might be strengthened for a while by the pressure of a radical trade union program. One must openly warn the workers of this. One must set about creating special defense organizations in a practical way right now. There is no other road! You can no more save yourself from fascism with the help of democratic laws, resolutions or proclamations than you can from a cavalry unit with the help of diplomatic notes. One must teach the workers to defend their lives and their future, arms in hand, from the gangsters and bandits of capital. Fascism grows swiftly in an atmosphere of immunity from punishment. One cannot doubt for a moment that the fascist heroes will turn with their tails between their legs when they realize that for each of their squadrons the workers are ready to send out two, three or four squadrons of their own. The only way to save not only the workers' organizations, but also to keep casualties to the minimum, is to create a powerful organization of workers' self-defense in time. This is the trade unions' most important responsibility, if they do not wish to perish ingloriously. The working class needs a *workers' militia!*

A: But what is the further perspective? Where will such methods of struggle get the trade unions in the last analysis?

B: It is obvious that the sliding scale and workers' self-defense are not sufficient. These are just the first steps, necessary in order to protect the workers from death by starvation or the fascists' knives. These are urgent and necessary means of self-defense. But by themselves they will not resolve the problem. The basic task consists in laying the foundation for a better economic system. for a more just, rational, and decent utilization of the productive forces in the interests of all the people.

This can't be attained by the ordinary, "normal," routine methods of the trade unions. You cannot disagree with this, for in the conditions of capitalist decline isolated unions turn out to be incapable of halting even the further deterioration of the workers' conditions. More decisive and deep-going methods are necessary. The bourgeoisie, who hold sway over the means of production and who have state power, have brought the economy to a state of total and hopeless disarray. It is necessary to declare the bourgeoisie incompetent and to transfer the economy into fresh and honest hands, that is, into the hands of the workers themselves. How to do this? The first step is clear: all the trade unions should unite and form their own *labor party.* Not the party of Roosevelt or La Guardia, not a "labor" party in name only, but a truly independent political organization of the working class. Only such a party is capable of gathering around itself the ruined farmers, the small artisans, the shopkeepers. But for this it would have to wage an uncompromising struggle against the banks, trusts, monopolies, and their political agents, that is, the Republican and Democratic parties. The task of the labor party should consist in taking power into its own hands, all the power, and then putting the economy in order. This means: to organize the entire national economy according to a single rational plan, whose aim is not the profit of a small bunch of exploiters, but the material and spiritual interests of a population of 130 million.

A: Many of our activists are beginning to understand that the course of political development is moving towards a labor party. But Roosevelt's popularity is still too great. If he agrees to run for president a third time, the question of a labor party will have to be postponed another four years.

B: There precisely is the tragedy resulting from the fact that Messrs. Leaders look to those above them instead of those below. The coming war, the decay of American capitalism, the growth of unemployment and poverty, all these basic processes, which directly determine the fate of dozens and hundreds of millions of people, do not depend on the candidacy or "popularity" of Roosevelt. I assure you that he is far more popular among the well-paid CIO officials than among the unemployed. Incidentally, the trade unions exist for the workers, not the officials. If the idea of the CIO inspired millions of workers for a certain period, the idea of an independent, militant labor party that aims to put an end to economic anarchy, unemployment, and misery, to save the people and its culture, the idea of such a party is capable of inspiring tens of millions. Of course, the agitators of the labor party would immediately have to show the masses, by word and deed, that they were not electoral agents of Roosevelt, La Guardia and Company, but true fighters for the interests of the exploited masses. When the speakers talk in the language of workers' leaders and not of White House agents, then 85 per cent of the members will come to meetings, while the 15 per cent of conservative oldsters, worker-aristocrats, and careerists will stay away. The masses are better, more daring, more resolute than the leaders. The masses wish to struggle. Putting the brakes on the struggle are the leaders who have lagged behind the masses. Their own indecisiveness, their own conservatism, their own bourgeois prejudices are disguised by the leaders with allusions to the backwardness of the masses. Such is the true state of affairs at present.

A: Now, what you say has a lot of truth in it.

B: But let's talk about that next time.

September 29, 1938

Trade Unions in the Epoch
Of Imperialist Decay

There is one common feature in the development, or more correctly the degeneration, of modern trade union organizations throughout the world: it is their drawing closely to and growing together with the state power. This process is equally characteristic of the neutral, the social-democratic, the Communist, and "anarchist" trade unions. This fact alone shows that the tendency towards "growing together" is intrinsic not in this or that doctrine as such but derives from social conditions common for all unions.

Monopoly capitalism does not rest on competition and free private initiative but on centralized command. The capitalist cliques at the head of mighty trusts, syndicates, banking consortiums, etc., view economic life from the very same heights as does state power; and they require at every step the collaboration of the latter. In their turn the trade unions in the most important branches of industry find themselves deprived of the possibility of profiting by the competition among the different enterprises. They have to confront a centralized capitalist adversary, intimately bound up with state power. Hence flows the need of the the trade unions — insofar as they remain on reformist positions, i.e., on positions of adapting themselves to private property — to adapt themselves to the capitalist state and to contend for its cooperation. In the eyes of the bureaucracy of the trade union movement, the chief task lies in "freeing" the state from the embrace of capitalism, in weakening its dependence on trusts, in pulling it over to their side. This position is in complete harmony with the social position of the labor aristocracy and the labor bureaucracy, who fight for a crumb in the share of superprofits of imperialist capitalism. The labor bureaucrats do their level best in words and deeds to demonstrate to the "democratic" state how reliable and indispensable they are in peacetime and especially in time of war. By transforming the trade unions into organs of the state, fascism invents nothing new; it merely draws to their ultimate conclusion the tendencies inherent in imperialism.

Colonial and semicolonial countries are under the sway, not of native capitalism but of foreign imperialism. However, this does not weaken but, on the contrary, strengthens the need of direct, daily, practical ties between the magnates of capitalism and the governments which are in essence subject to them — the governments of colonial or semicolonial countries. Inasmuch as imperialist capitalism creates both in colonies and semicolonies a stratum of labor aristocracy and bureaucracy, the latter requires the support of colonial and semicolonial governments as protectors, patrons, and sometimes as arbitrators. This constitutes the most important social basis for the Bonapartist and semi-Bonapartist[58] character of governments in the colonies and in backward countries generally. This likewise constitutes the basis for the dependence of reformist unions upon the state.

In Mexico the trade unions have been transformed by law into semistate institutions and have, in the nature of things, assumed a semitotalitarian character. The statization of the trade unions was, according to the conception of the legislators, introduced in the interests of the workers, in order to assure them an influence upon governmental and economic life. But insofar as foreign imperialist capitalism dominates the national state and insofar as it is able, with the assistance of internal reactionary forces, to overthrow the unstable democracy and replace it with outright fascist dictatorship, to that extent the legislation relating to the trade unions can easily become a weapon in the hands of imperialist dictatorship.

From the foregoing it seems, at first sight, easy to draw the conclusion that the trade unions cease to be trade unions in the imperialist epoch. They leave almost no room at all for workers' democracy which, in the good old days when free trade ruled on the economic arena, constituted the content of the inner life of labor organization. In the absence of workers' democracy there cannot be any free struggle for influence over the trade union membership. And because of this, the chief arena of work for revolutionists within the trade unions disappears. Such a position, however, would be false to the core. We cannot select the arena and the conditions for our activity to suit our own likes and dislikes. It is infinitely more difficult to fight in a totalitarian or a semitotalitarian state for influence over the working masses than in a democracy. The very same thing likewise applies to trade unions whose fate reflects the change in the destiny of capitalist states. We cannot renounce the struggle for influence over workers in Germany merely because the totalitarian regime makes such work extremely difficult there. We cannot, in precisely the same way, renounce the struggle within the compulsory labor organizations created by fascism. All the less so can we renounce internal systematic work in trade unions of totalitarian and semitotalitarian type merely because they depend directly or indirectly on the workers' state or because the bureaucracy deprives the revolutionists of the possibility of working freely within these trade unions. It is necessary to conduct a struggle under all those concrete conditions which have been created by the preceding developments, including therein the mistakes of the working class and the crimes of its leaders. In the fascist and semifascist countries it is impossible to carry on revolutionary work that is not underground, illegal, conspiratorial. Within the totalitarian and semitotalitarian unions it is impossible or well-nigh impossible to carry on any except conspiratorial work. It is necessary to adapt ourselves to the concrete conditions existing in the trade unions of every given country in order to mobilize the masses, not only against the bourgeoisie, but also against the totalitarian regime within the trade unions themselves and against the leaders enforcing this regime. The primary slogan for this struggle is: *complete and unconditional independence of the trade unions in relation to the capitalist state.* This means a struggle to turn the trade unions into the organs of the broad exploited masses and not the organs of a labor aristocracy.

*   *   *

The second slogan is: *trade union democracy.* This second slogan flows directly from the first and presupposes for its realization the complete freedom of the trade unions from the imperialist or colonial state.

In other words, the trade unions in the present epoch cannot simply be the organs of democracy as they were in the epoch of free capitalism and they cannot any longer remain politically neutral, that is, limit themselves to serving the daily needs of the working class. They cannot any longer be anarchistic, i.e., ignore the decisive influence of the state on the life of people and classes. They can no longer be reformist, because the objective conditions leave no room for any serious and lasting reforms. The trade unions of our time can either serve as secondary instruments of imperialist capitalism for the subordination and disciplining of workers and for obstructing the revolution, or, on the contrary, the trade unions can become the instruments of the revolutionary movement of the proletariat.

*   *   *

The neutrality of trade unions is completely and irretrievably a thing of the past — gone, together with the free bourgeois democracy.

*   *   *

From what has been said it follows quite clearly that, in spite of the progressive degeneration of trade unions and their growing together with the imperialist state, the work within the trade unions not only does not lose any of its importance but remains as before and becomes in a certain sense even more important work than ever for every revolutionary party. The matter at issue is essentially the struggle for influence over the working class. Every organization, every party, every faction which permits itself an ultimatistic[59] position in relation to the trade union, i.e., in essence turns its back upon the working class, merely because of displeasure with its organization, every such organization is destined to perish. And it must be said it deserves to perish.

*   *   *

Inasmuch as the chief role in backward countries is not played by national but by foreign capitalism, the national bourgeoisie occupies, in the sense of its social position, a much more minor position than corresponds with the development of industry. Inasmuch as foreign capital does not import workers but proletarianizes the native population, the national proletariat soon begins playing the most important role in the life of the country. In these conditions the national government, to the extent that it tries to show resistance to foreign capital, is compelled to a greater or lesser degree to lean on the proletariat. On the other hand, the governments of those backward countries which consider it inescapable or more profitable for themselves to march shoulder to shoulder with foreign capital, destroy the labor organizations and institute a more or less totalitarian regime. Thus, the feebleness of the national bourgeoisie, the absence of traditions of municipal self-government, the pressure of foreign capitalism, and the relatively rapid growth of the proletariat, cut the ground from under any kind of stable democratic regime. The governments of backward, i.e., colonial and semicolonial, countries by and large assume a Bonapartist or semi-Bonapartist character; they differ from one another in that some try to orient in a democratic direction, seeking support among workers and peasants, while others install a form close to military-police dictatorship. This likewise determines the fate of the trade unions. They either stand under the special patronage of the state or they are subjected to cruel persecution. Patronage on the part of the state is dictated by two tasks that confront it: first, to draw the working class closer, thus gaining a support for resistance against excessive pretensions on the part of imperialism; and, at the same time, to discipline the workers themselves by placing them under the control of a bureaucracy.

*　　*　　*

Monopoly capitalism is less and less willing to reconcile itself to the independence of trade unions. It demands of the reformist bureaucracy and the labor aristocracy, who pick up the crumbs from its banquet table, that they become transformed into its political police before the eyes of the working class. If that is not achieved, the labor bureaucracy is driven away and replaced by the fascists. Incidentally, all the efforts of the labor aristocracy in the service of imperialism cannot in the long run save them from destruction.

The intensification of class contradictions within each country, the intensification of antagonisms between one country and another, produce a situation in which imperialist capitalism can tolerate (i.e., up to a certain time) a reformist bureaucracy only if the latter serves directly as a petty but active stockholder of its imperialist enterprises, of its plans and programs within the country as well as on the world arena. Social reformism must become transformed into social imperialism in order to prolong its existence, but only prolong it, and nothing more. Because along this road there is no way out in general.

Does this mean that in the epoch of imperialism independent trade unions are generally impossible? It would be fundamentally incorrect to pose the question this way. Impossible are the independent or semi-independent reformist trade unions. Wholly possible are revolutionary trade unions which not only are not stockholders of imperialist policy but which set as their task the direct overthrow of the rule of capitalism. In the epoch of imperialist decay the trade unions can be really independent only to the extent that they are conscious of being, in action, the organs of proletarian revolution. In this sense, the program of transitional demands adopted by the last congress of the Fourth International is not only the program for the activity of the party but in its fundamental features it is the program for activity of the trade unions.

*　　*　　*

The development of backward countries is characterized by its combined character. In other words, the last word of imperialist technology, economics, and politics is combined in these countries with traditional backwardness and primitiveness. This law can be observed in the most diverse spheres of the development of colonial and semicolonial countries, including the sphere of the trade union movement. Imperialist capitalism operates here in its most cynical and naked form. It transports to virgin soil the most perfected methods of its tyrannical rule.

*　　*　　*

In the trade union movement throughout the world there is to be observed in the last period a swing to the right and the suppression of internal democracy. In England, the Minority Movement in the trade unions has been crushed (not without the assistance of Moscow); the leaders of the trade union movement are today, especially in the field of foreign policy, the obedient agents of the Conservative Party. In France there was no room for an independent existence for Stalinist trade unions; they united with the so-called anarcho-syndicalist trade unions under the leadership of Jouhaux, and as a result of this unification there was a general shift of the trade union movement not to the left but to the right. The leadership of the CGT is the most direct and open agency of French imperialist capitalism.

In the United States the trade union movement has passed through the most stormy history in recent years. The rise of the CIO is incontrovertible evidence of the revolutionary tendencies within the working masses. Indicative and noteworthy in the highest degree, however, is the fact that the new "leftist" trade union organization was no sooner founded than it fell into the steel embrace of the imperialist state. The struggle among the tops between the old federation and the new[60] is reducible in large measure to the struggle for the sympathy and support of Roosevelt and his cabinet.

No less graphic, although in a different sense, is the picture of the development or the degeneration of the trade union movement in Spain. In the socialist trade unions all those leading elements which to any degree represented the independence of the trade union movement were pushed out. As regards the anarcho-syndicalist unions, they were transformed into the instrument of the bourgeois republicans; the anarcho-syndicalist leaders became conservative bourgeois ministers. The fact that this metamorphosis took place in conditions of civil war does not weaken its significance. War is the continuation of the self-same policies. It speeds up processes, exposes their basic features, destroys all that is rotten, false, equivocal, and lays bare all that is essential. The shift of the trade unions to the right was due to the sharpening of class and international contradictions. The leaders of the trade union movement sensed or understood, or were given to understand, that now was no time to play the game of opposition. Every oppositional movement within the trade union movement, especially among the tops, threatens to provoke a stormy movement of the masses and to create difficulties for national imperialism. Hence flows the swing of the trade unions to the right and the suppression of workers' democracy within the unions. The basic feature, the swing towards the totalitarian regime, passes through the labor movement of the whole world.

We should also recall Holland, where the reformist and the trade union movement was not only a reliable prop of imperialist capitalism, but where the so-called anarcho-syndicalist organization also was actually under the control of the imperialist government. The secretary of this organization, Sneevliet, in spite of his platonic sympathies for the Fourth International, was as deputy in the Dutch Parliament most concerned lest the wrath of the government descend upon his trade union organization.

*   *   *

In the United States the Department of Labor with its leftist bureaucracy has as its task the subordination of the trade union movement to the democratic state, and it must be said that this task has up to now been solved with some success.

*   *   *

The nationalization of railways and oil fields in Mexico has, of course, nothing in common with socialism. It is a measure of state capitalism in a backward country which in this way seeks to defend itself on the one hand against foreign imperialism and on the other against its own proletariat. The management of railways, oil fields, etc., through labor organizations has nothing in common with workers' control over industry, for in the essence of the matter the management is effected through the labor bureaucracy which is independent of the workers but, in return, completely dependent on the bourgeois state. This measure on the part of the ruling class pursues the aim of disciplining the working class, making it more industrious in the service of the common interests of the state, which appear on the surface to merge with the interests of the working class itself. As a matter of fact, the whole task of the bourgeoisie consists in liquidating the trade unions as organs of the class struggle and substituting in their place the trade union bureaucracy as the organ of the leadership over the workers by the bourgeois state. In these conditions, the task of the revolutionary vanguard is to conduct a struggle for the complete independence of the trade unions and for the introduction of actual workers' control over the present union bureaucracy, which has been turned into the administration of railways, oil enterprises, and so on.

*   *   *

Events of the last period (before the war) have revealed with especial clarity that anarchism, which in point of theory is always only liberalism drawn to its extremes, was, in practice, peaceful propaganda within the democratic republic, the protection of which it required. If we leave aside individual terrorist acts, etc., anarchism, as a system of mass movement and politics, presented only propaganda material under the peaceful protection of the laws. In conditions of crisis the anarchists always did the opposite of what they taught in peacetimes. This was pointed out by Marx himself in connection with the Paris Commune. And it was repeated on a far more colossal scale in the experience of the Spanish Revolution.

*   *   *

Democratic unions in the old sense of the term — bodies where, in the framework of one and the same mass organization, different tendencies struggle more or less freely — can no longer exist. Just as it is impossible to bring back the bourgeois-democratic state, so is it impossible to bring back the old workers' democracy. The fate of the one reflects the fate of the other. As a matter of fact, the independence of the trade unions in the class sense, in their relations to the bourgeois state, can, in the present conditions, be assured only by a completely revolutionary leadership, that is, the leadership of the Fourth International. This leadership, naturally, must and can be rational and assure the unions the maximum of democracy conceivable under the present concrete conditions. But without the political leadership of the Fourth International the independence of the trade unions is impossible.

NOTES

1. **Louzon**, Robert (1882-   ). Revolutionary syndicalist, at that time member of the Communist Party of France. He and Monatte were to follow the same path together, both winding up in the **Révolution prolétarienne** group. Trotsky had temporarily put aside his differences with Monatte and Louzon to concentrate his efforts on the struggle against Frossard.

2. **Fourth World Congress of the Communist International**. November-December 1922. At this congress, Trotsky reported on the crisis in the French party.

3. **Frossard**, Louis-Olivier (1889-1946). Left centrist. Secretary of the CPF after 1920, resigned in 1923 and rejoined the Socialist Party. Quit SP in 1935 to become Minister of Labor. Minister in the Popular Front governments and in first Pétain government.

4. **Monatte**, Pierre (1881-1960). Revolutionary syndicalist, founded **Vie ouvrière** in 1909. One of the first to oppose World War I. Joined the CPF in 1923, only to leave a year later. Founded **Révolution prolétarienne** in 1924 and the Syndicalist League in 1926.

5. **Red International of Labor Unions**. Also known as the **Profintern**, from the combination of its Russian initials. It was founded in Moscow in 1921 as a rival to the reformist ("yellow") international labor federation whose headquarters were in Amsterdam.

6. **Lassalle**, Ferdinand (1825-1864). German socialist; he organized the General Union of German Workers in 1863. Its fusion with the German followers of Marx ultimately produced the Social Democratic Party.

7. **Vie ouvrière**. See note 4.

8. **Jouhaux**, Léon (1870-1954). Leader of **Confédération Générale du Travail** (CGT) and its secretary general from 1921 until second world war. Social-patriotic syndicalist during first world war. Opponent of Russian Revolution. For Trotsky, he was the personification of class collaborationism.

9. **The "Pact."** Signed by eighteen anarchists and semianarchists in February 1921, its existence was kept secret. Permeated with the spirit of freemasonry and "pure syndicalism," its signers aimed to take and keep hold of the trade union movement in France as against the leadership of the Communists. Its revelation some time before the founding convention (June 1922) of the **Confédération Générale du Travail Unitaire** (CGTU) created a stir. The pact failed in its aim, as the CGTU chose the leadership of the Communists and syndicalist-communists.

10. **Le Temps**. Leading French newspaper between World Wars I and II; regarded as semiofficial voice of the government; very corrupt; banned after World War II for collaboration with the fascists.

11. **Eisenach**. Wilhelm Liebknecht and August Bebel, German followers of Marx, founded the Social Democratic Labor Party in 1869 in Eisenach as a rival to the Lassallist General Union of German Workers. The Lassallists and the Eisenachers finally united their movements in 1875 at a convention in Gotha. See note 6.

12. **Louzon's new article**. See **International Press Correspondence**, June 14, 1923.

13. **CGT**. Confédération Générale du Travail (General Confederation of Labor), the reformist trade union confederation led by Jouhaux.

14. **Renaudel**, Pierre (1871-1935). Right-hand man to socialist leader Jean Jaurès before 1914; social-patriotic editor of l'**Humanité** during World War I; subsequently a leader of right wing in Socialist Party.

15. **Jouhaux . . . and their like**. For Jouhaux, see note 8. **Dumoulin**, Georges (1877-1963). Centrist during World War I; later joined Jouhaux and right wing; held various union posts before World War II when he collaborated with Vichy government. **Merrheim**, Alphonse (1871-1923). Supporter of Jouhaux in 1917; fought the revolutionaries and remained in right wing of the CGT after the 1921 split.

16. **Blum-Renaudel party**. The Socialist Party. **Léon Blum** (1872-1950) was editor of the principal Socialist newspaper, **Le Populaire**. After the 1936 elections, he became premier of the first Popular Front government. For **Renaudel**, see note 14.

17. **Epigones**. Disciples who corrupt the doctrines of their teacher.

18. **Brandler group**. Followers of Heinrich Brandler, leader of the German Communist Party who was expelled in 1928-29 when the Comintern took its ultraleft zigzag. The Brandlerites had international ties with the American Lovestone group and other former collaborators of Bukharin, i.e., the Right Opposition in the Communist movement.

19. **Cachin, Monmousseau and Company**. **Marcel Cachin** (1869-1958), an ardent social-patriot during World War I, came over to communism in 1920. He became an unswerving Stalinist and retained the editorship of l'**Humanité** until his death. **Gaston Monmousseau** (1883-1960), a former revolutionary syndicalist, became a CP and CGTU leader and a staunch Stalinist.

20. **Rosmer**, Alfred (1877-1964). Originally an anarchist, then a syndicalist, he engaged in agitation against World War I, collaborating with Trotsky in this until the latter's expulsion from France. A founding member of the French Communist Party, he was elected to the Executive Committee of the Comintern. Expelled from the CP in 1924; a member of the Trotskyist movement from its beginning to his resignation in 1930. He remained a close personal friend of Trotsky and Natalia Sedova (Trotsky's widow).

21. **Guesdists**. Followers in the socialist movement of Jules Guesde (1845-1922), first Marxist leader in France and Jaurès' rival in the unified party. Guesde prided himself on his strict Marxist orthodoxy, but he became a social-patriot during World War I.

22. **Third Republic**. The government of France from the end of the Second Empire (1871) till the Nazi invasion and the establishment of the Vichy regime (1940).

23. **Proudhonism**. The school of thought originated by Pierre-Joseph Proudhon (1809-1865), the famous utopian socialist. He envisioned a society based on fair exchange between independent producers and considered the state less important than the workshops which he believed would replace it.

24. **Quai de Jemmapes**. The headquarters of **Vie ouvrière**, Monatte's former newspaper, was located there.

25. **Amiens Charter**. Adopted under the influence of syndicalists at the Amiens congress (1906) of the CGT, it demanded the complete autonomy and absolute independence of the unions from political parties.

26. **Anglo-Russian Committee**. Formed in May 1925 with equal representation from the leaderships of the British and Russian trade union federations. It served the British labor leaders as a left cover against Communist Party criticism while they sold out the British General Strike of

1926. When they had no further advantage to derive from it, the British labor leaders quit the committee.

27. **Révolution prolétarienne.** Syndicalist newspaper founded by Monatte in 1924, after he had left the Communist Party.

28. [**Lenin's**] **testament.** Lenin's letter of December 25, 1922, with a postscript dated January 4, 1923, proposing to the Soviet Communist Party that Stalin be removed from the post of General Secretary. Its existence was long denied by the Stalinists but was officially revealed by Khrushchev in the period of de-Stalinization. (Available from Merit Publishers.)

29. **Amsterdam.** See note 5.

30. **Monatte Crosses the Rubicon.** Monatte and his friends of the Syndicalist League had issued a declaration, "For the Reconstruction of Trade Union Unity." Signed by twenty-two activists of the CGT, CGTU, and independent unions, and including Georges Dumoulin (see note 15), the declaration affirmed: "Some trade union activists . . . have agreed that, after ten years of fratricidal struggle, it was necessary to make an effort to put an end to the split in the trade unions. They have agreed to launch the idea of reestablishing trade union unity in a single central organization, on the basis of the Amiens Charter. In their opinion this can come about only on the basis of the class struggle and of the independence of the trade union movement, without any interference from political parties, factions, and sects, as well as from governments." (**Révolution prolétarienne,** No. 112, December 5, 1930.)

31. **Sebastian Faure** . . . **Malvy.** In January 1915, **Faure** called for a struggle against the war. Shortly thereafter, he made a deal with Minister of the Interior **Malvy** renouncing antiwar agitation.

32. **French Bourse.** Stock exchange.

33. **Chambelland,** Maurice (1901-1966). On editorial staff of **Vie ouvrière** in 1922, in Communist Party in 1923, editor on staff of **l'Humanité**. Resigned from the paper and from the CPF in 1924. Member of the **Révolution prolétarienne** group. Monatte's closest assistant.

34. **Execution of Indochinese revolutionists.** Following a mutiny in the garrison at Yen Bai in February 1930, there were local peasant uprisings and then strikes which reached their peak in the big cities in May. French imperialist reprisals were savage, with thousands shot, tens of thousands arrested, and thousands of houses burned.

35. **Zyromsky,** Jean (1890-   ). Leader of left wing in French Socialist Party in the nineteen-thirties. During World War II he joined the Communist Party.

36. **MacDonald,** James Ramsay (1866-1937). Pacifist socialist during World War I. First Labour Prime Minister of Great Britain (1924). In 1931, during his second term as Prime Minister, he deserted the Labour Party to form a "national unity" cabinet with the Conservative Party.

37. **Curzon,** George Nathaniel, Lord (1859-1925). British Minister of Foreign Affairs from 1919 to 1923.

38. **Thomas,** J.H. (1874-1949). British trade union leader. Colonial Secretary in Labour Party government of 1924. Deserted Labour Party along with MacDonald in 1931, when he was again given Colonial Secretaryship.

39. **Louis Sellier** (1885-   ). General Secretary of French Communist Party after Frossard's resignation in 1923; quit party in 1929; founded the POP (Parti Ouvrier et Paysan — Workers and Peasants Party). The POPists were the French equivalent of the Brandlerites in Germany and the Lovestoneites in the U.S.

40. **Versailles.** The Treaty of Versailles was imposed on Germany at the end of World War I by the victorious allied imperialists.

41. **Kuomintang.** Nationalist bourgeois party founded by Sun Yat-sen, leader of First Chinese Revolution (1911). In the Second Chinese Revolution (1925-27), the Stalin-Bukharin line forced the Chinese Communists to dissolve their party and enter the Kuomintang, which was admitted to the Comintern as a sympathizing party in 1926. After using the Kuomintang to restrain and hobble

the revolution, Chiang Kai-shek finally was able, in March 1927, to launch one of the worst massacres in modern history against the Communists and the revolutionary workers and peasants.

42. **Purcell, Hicks, Cook.** "Left" trade union officials in Great Britain. **A.A. Purcell** and **George Hicks** were on the General Council of the Trade Union Congress; **A.J. Cook** was secretary of the miners' federation.

43. **Stalin . . . and Company.** Nikolai Bukharin (1888-1938), Bolshevik leader; head of Comintern from 1926 to 1929; "confessed" at third Moscow Trial and was executed in 1938. (See note 18.) **A. Losovsky** was head of the Red International of Labor Unions. (See note 5.)

44. **Lovestoneites.** Followers of Jay Lovestone, head of the Communist Party of the U.S. who carried out the expulsion of the American Trotskyists in 1928. Stalin summarily deposed him in 1929 as part of the international purge of the Right Opposition, collaborators of Bukharin. The Lovestoneites maintained an independent organization until the outbreak of World War II, when they disbanded. Lovestone became an anti-Communist expert for the union bureaucracy and the "grey eminence" of AFL-CIO President George Meany's ultraright foreign policy.

45. **La Vérité.** Newspaper of the Communist League, the French Trotskyist organization.

46. **POPists.** See note 39.

47. **Unitary.** The name taken by the left-wing union confederation in France was **Confédération Générale du Travail Unitaire** (CGTU), whereas the name of the right-wing confederation was **Confédération Générale du Travail** (CGT).

48. **Vassart,** Albert (1898-1958). One of the Communist Party leaders in the red trade unions who, after having been an ardent ultraleftist during the "third period," disputed CP policy. Sometimes in their polemics, CP leaders labeled Vassart's positions as "semi-Trotskyist."

49. **Losovsky, Manuilsky and Company.** A. Losovsky, see notes 5 and 43. **Dmitri Manuilsky** (1883-1959) was head of the Comintern from 1929 to 1934, i.e., during the "third period."

50. **"Third period."** According to a Stalinist schema of history, this was the final period of capitalism, the period of its immediately impending demise and replacement by soviets. It was marked by ultraleft and adventurist tactics on the part of the Communists.

51. **Profintern.** See note 5.

52. **Social-fascism.** One of the most disastrous inventions of the "third period." Following Stalin's dictum that the socialists and fascists were not antagonists "but twins," the Communist line throughout the world dubbed the social democratic parties and unions "social-fascist" and, accordingly, a greater danger than the true fascists. This made a united front against Nazism and other fascist movements impossible.

53. **Citrine,** Sir Walter (1887-   ). General Secretary of the British Trades Union Congress (1926-1946). Knighted for his services to British capitalism in 1935, made a baronet in 1946.

54. **Mosley, Sir Oswald** (1896-   ). Head of the British Union of Fascists and National Socialists.

55. **RSAP.** Revolutionair Socialistische Arbeiders Partij (Revolutionary Socialist Workers Party). After quitting the Communist Party in 1927, Sneevliet (see note 57) organized the Revolutionary Socialist Party. This party rallied to the movement for a Fourth International in 1934 and the following year fused with other revolutionary elements in Holland to form the RSAP. Because of differences on trade union policy and attitude towards the POUM in Spain, the RSAP broke with the international Trotskyist movement and did not participate in the founding congress of the Fourth International in 1938.

Two tendencies developed in the RSAP, which split in 1942. One, led by Sneevliet, followed the lines of traditional Dutch ultraleftism. It published the paper **Spartacus.** The other, Committee of Revolutionary Marxists, developed to the positions of the Fourth International. It published the paper **De Rode October.** Both papers were published illegally during the Nazi occupation, and both groups cooperated in fighting the German fascists and their Dutch quislings.

56. **NAS.** Nationaal Arbeids Secretariaat (National Labor Organization), founded in 1893, dissolved in July 1940 at the beginning of the Nazi occupation of Holland; it was not reconstituted after World War II.

The NAS stood as a small revolutionary rival to the NVV, the big reformist-led union organization. Those explaining the Dutch labor scene to Americans find it useful to draw an analogy between the NAS and the Industrial Workers of the World. During the nineteen-thirties, the highly militant and class-conscious membership of the NAS consisted largely of longshoremen and construction workers. It had had a large section of municipal workers in Amsterdam prior to 1934, when the government forbade such employees to belong to the "red" union. To understand Trotsky's statement, further on in the text, that "The NAS exists only thanks to the toleration and financial support of the bourgeois government," it must be kept in mind that the Dutch government's unemployment dole was distributed to jobless workers through their trade union organizations, including the NAS.

57. **Sneevliet**, Henricus (1883-1942). The outstanding revolutionary socialist leader in Holland and the first builder of a proletarian Marxist movement in Indonesia.

A tramway worker and left socialist, he was elected president of the railway and tramway workers' union in 1909. He resigned this post and went to the Dutch East Indies (Indonesia) in 1912 as the consequence of a dispute with the reformist leadership of the NVV, the big labor federation, over the latter's refusal to support a seamen's strike. In Indonesia he carried on a brilliant campaign of political and trade union organization until he was deported at the end of 1917 for calling upon the Indonesians to follow the example of the Bolsheviks in Russia.

Back in Holland, he was a co-founder of the Communist Party; subsequently he was sent by the Communist International (under the name **Maring**) to do revolutionary work in China, where he established contact with Sun Yat-sen.

After his return to Holland, he was elected president of the NAS. In 1933 he was imprisoned for solidarity actions with the mutineers in the Dutch navy. Upon his release, he was elected to parliament.

During the Nazi occupation of Holland, Sneevliet and seven comrades were arrested, tried, and executed by firing squad at the Amersfoort concentration camp on April 13, 1942. Among his statements on his last day was the following:"Friends, we are proud to be the first in the Netherlands to be condemned before a tribunal for the cause of the International and who must therefore die for this cause." Sneevliet conducted himself with great courage. He requested that he and his comrades be allowed to face the firing squad holding hands. This was refused. Then he requested that they not be blindfolded and that, as the oldest and their political leader, he be shot last. This was granted.

58. **Bonapartist and semi-Bonapartist**. Bonapartism is a Marxist term describing a dictatorship, or a regime with certain features of dictatorship, based on the military, police and state bureaucracy rather than on the parliamentary parties or a mass movement; usually a "strong-man" regime which, in a period of crisis or stalemate of contending class forces, elevates itself to a seeming independence of, and superiority to, the nation's classes.

59. **Ultimatistic**. The political vice of announcing slogans, programs or positions to the masses as ultimatums, i.e., in a peremptory, take-it-or-else manner, regardless of the workers' level of understanding or desires on the subject at issue.

60. **Old Federation and the new**. The old American Federation of Labor (AFL) and the newly founded Congress of Industrial Organizations (CIO).